Luke Limner

[ZHINGOORA BOOKS]

This edition is published by
Zhingoora Books.

The Cover is Designed by Pallav Sethiya.

Contents

THE CAROL.
"TIDINGS OF COMFORT & JOY."

CHRISTMAS.

COMES BUT ONCE A YEAR

ERY cold, very bleak; the thermometer and snow are falling fast; eggs and suet are rising faster; everything at this season is "prized," and everybody apprizes everybody else of the good they wish them,—"A Merry Christmas and a Happy New Year!" Even the shivering caroller, for "it is a poor heart that never rejoices," is yelling forth the "tidings of comfort and joy." The snow that descends, making park and common alike— topping palace and pigsty, now crowns the semi-detached villas, Victoria and Albert. They were erected from the designs of John Brown, Esq. and his architect (or builder), and are considered a fine specimen of compo-cockney-gothic, in which the constructor has made the most of his materials; for, to save digging, he sank the foundation in an evacuated pond, and, as an antidote to damp, used wood with the dry-rot—the little remaining moisture being pumped out daily by the domestics. The floors are delightfully springy, having cracks to precipitate the dirt, and are sloped towards the doorways, so that the furniture is perpetually trying to walk out of the rooms; but those apertures are ingeniously planned to prevent the evil—the doors obstinately refusing to open at all, without force. That the whole may not appear too light, few windows are introduced. By casual observers the Victoria and Albert would be taken for one—so united are they; and had we not seen the parting division, we should have doubted also. Of the entrance lodges, we have noticed one of the chimneys smoking periodically; and, from the mollient white vapour issuing over the window at such times, presume Victoria is washing, whilst Albert is locked up and doing nothing.

Their lord and master is John Brown, Esq., Director of the Deptford Direct, the Stag Assurance, and Churchwarden of this parish—St. Stiff the Martyr,—a portly upright man; for had he not been so erect, to balance a "fair round belly," he would have toppled on his nose. Everybody said that he was clever, too—and, moreover, always thought so; for luck had made our friend a rising man amongst the suburban aristocracy of Mizzlington. Of Mrs. Brown, she is his match, and portly too; though older and more crusty—a crummy dame, to whom her lord must bow; for, upon his hinting at duty, and an obedient wife's *commanding* her husband, she ordered him off, reading the adage as a womanought. Of the Misses Brown, Jemima and Angelina, they are decidedly getting old—for young ladies, having been "out" for some time; and, like the back numbers of an old periodical, are not the more interesting or marketable for it. Of the sons, the elder, John Brown, jun., is spoiling himself by patronising all that is "fast;" whilst the younger is being educated for a faster age, being spoilt first by his mother.

Having characterised the Brown family, we will now introduce you to the first scene of this domestic drama. Victoria Villa—a dormitory—midnight; in the back ground may be seen and heard a lady in a rich mellow snore, whilst distant music—the Christmas Waits, is "softly o'er the senses stealing," and loud in the promise of "a good time coming," provided you will "wait a little longer." Mr. Brown is seated at the dressing-table, making up his Diary, or rather trying to cram the events of twenty-four hours into the leaf of a pocket-book, five and a half inches by three and a quarter—his usual custom before rest:—

THE WAITS.

"SOFTLY O'ER THE SENSES STEALING."

"December 21st, *Friday.*—Advertised in this day's 'Times,' to let Albert, furnished, from the 25th, with use of servants, if required (double-house and household at half-price—grand effect united with economy). Tommy came home from Dr. Tortem's, with holiday-letter, bill, and wonderful crop of hair—considering it costs me five shillings per quarter to cut; brimstone and treacle, under head—medicine, charged ten and six; firing and broken windows, two pounds; &c.:—what most unlucky things turn up on a Friday! I much wish I had not advertised Albert to-day—no one will come." With these observations, and a consolatory grumble about Christmas coming but once a year, Mr. Brown seeks repose beside his consort; whilst the Waits make the lowing wind, the frigid vegetation, and the rattling shutters, dance again to the "Bridal Polka."

Sweet sleep—and morning dawns.—The Browns depart, as is their daily custom, by the omnibus—the elder to chat inside, the younger to smoke out;—and both to business in the city. Whilst, at home, Master Tommy displays the "advancement made in his studies"—as the holiday-letter states,—by practising writing in

the "Book of Beauty;" his knowledge of natural history, by attempting to rear gold-fish (like eels) in sand; searching for the tick in an eight-day clock; setting bits of raw beef in the back garden, that the portion (like potatoes) might grow to young bullocks; filling the bellows' snout with gunpowder, that they may blow the fire up; putting the cat in walnut-shells upon the icy pond, and himself in the middle of it; playing racket in the drawing-room; and constructing a snow man against the back-door to fall in upon Sarah, almost frightening her to death; and many other experimental, philosophical tricks, too numerous to mention.

During this day the semi-detached is besieged by a lady and gentleman in search of a home. The gentleman, dressed in a very tight frock-coat, dusty and worn; a highly-glazed cap, the strap of which dangled above a tuft of hair, that graced his chin, its peak resting upon the tip of his nose, affording him little more than a view of his boots, with a portion of the hose protruding therefrom; his tightly-strapped trowsers carrying a broad stripe, of which he appeared proud, being engaged in the manufacture of many more in other parts, by knocking the dust out of them with a   slight

cane;   of   his gloves, they seemed determined to end their days in their normal state, and to produce neither mits nor finger-stalls. The couple looking very limp and tumbled;—a thing duly apologised for, and not to be wondered at—having just arrived from abroad. Mrs. Brown being much taken with the gentleman—for he curried favour by stroking only the way of the grain. So, with Lady Lucretia, Captain de Camp, of the Hon. East India Company's Service, from Madras—awaiting his luggage,—is at home in the

Albert, having given himself a character that satisfied Mrs. Brown; for, he omitted the objectionable parts (fearing they might distress that good lady), like the woman with a large family, who, finding it impossible to get lodgings, sent her children among the graves; that, when asked, she might say, with a sigh, "Alas! they are all in the churchyard."

That evening Mrs. Brown's rich mellow snore commenced later than usual—for she had been loud and long in the praise of their new neighbours. Mr. Brown making entry against December 22nd, *Saturday*.—That Albert was let:—whilst, the Waits were playing the "Phantom Dancers," and Captain de Camp busy, there, screwing his empty trunk to the floor, that it might appear heavy, and full of valuables; and whilst, between the villas in the rear, there might be seen a glimmering candle, and by that light be found—one not unknown to Brown—a poor little musician, in a little second-floor room, containing a little organ much too large for it, and a litter of dirty soft papers,—who is not a little perplexed at a note, from Mrs. Brown, dispensing with his services:—he, the poor little music-master, more amiable than handsome, less symmetrical than serviceable;—who had, in less favoured times, contracted friendship, and to teach the Misses Brown music at thirty shillings per quarter—who had gotten so familiar as to love—had dared to offer that person Nature had deformed, with that mind Nature had adorned, to Miss Jemima Brown. There was a time when his anecdotes had been prized, and his long, delicate, white fingers kept playing to perpetual dancers; and that fine voice, Nature had bestowed in lieu of symmetry, sang the merriest and most sentimental songs for love:—the retrospect is too much for poor Spohf—so he seeks refuge in his organ, much to the annoyance of a little tailor in the attic, who has no soul in him—save the sole he had for supper.

Sunday.—The perpetual bell of St. Stiff the Martyr is calling to service, as it is wont to do at all times and hours—for mysterious purposes but little known:—it seems as if the bell disliked its little wooden cottage, on the unfinished spire; or was inspired, or in a towering passion to live in a tower, or saw no fun in waiting for funds; and so, continually pealed an appeal to the public:—however, it was a puny, little, curious bell, with a tongue of its own, now clacking for a charity sermon; and, curiously, Mr. Brown thinks a charity sermon always edifies him with the headache, and is doubtful about going, as they make him a reluctant giver—for mere vain show; but he, curiously, wonders where the De Camps go; and, curiously, Victoria and Albert meet at the gate; and, curiously, the family pue, at St. Stiff's, seems capable of accommodating them.

Mr. Spohf, the little organist, being perched up aloft, sees, through the curtain, the Christmas holly and the Captain—taking care to mark that individual with mental chalk. The musician's eyes are in the Brown pue; but the eyes that used to meet them are turned another way—all favour is centred upon their spurious exotic, who grows thicker, twines tighter, and takes deeper root, the more he is encouraged:—of the species, or genus, we cannot do better than quote Mr. B.'s own words, written against December 23rd, *Sunday*—(whilst the Waits, as usual, were serenading the semi-detached, in a full conviction of its being Monday, and the possibility of "living and loving together," and "being happy yet").—"To church with my new tenant, who is delightful company: Lady Lucre. says he is a 'refined duck,' a 'gentlemanly angel,' and a 'manly poppet:' to which I made answer, that I thought so too; and that she was a 'seraphine concert.' Sermon, by the Rev. Loyalla à Becket, 'in aid of funds for supplying the poor, during this inclement but festive season, with food for the mind.' Captain de Camp did borrow a sovereign of me, to put in the plate; and I was told by my fellow-churchwarden, Mr. Flyntflayer, that he did put in a bad shilling, wrapt in paper, and did take out fifteen shillings in change:—this, I said was untrue—as, of course, it was;—having lent him a sovereign myself, for the express purpose. We are to have Captain de C.'s two noble sons here, during the holidays; one, I believe, comes from Oxford, and the other from Sandboys Military College:—now is the time—Jemy. and Angel. must be on the alert, for

'There is a tide in the affairs of *women,*

Which, taken at the flood, leads on to *matrimony*;

Omitted, all the voyage of their life

Is bound in shallows, and in *spinsterhood*.

On such a full sea are we now afloat;

And we must take the current when it serves,

Or lose our ventures.'"

Monday, the 24th December's sun rises in a fog:—everybody has lost the day of the week, and come upon what appears an infinity of Saturdays rolled into one—beginning the week with a grand end,—for it is the advent of Christmas!

The Masters de Camp arrive as was expected.—Cadet Wellesley exhibiting his military accomplishments by surveying the back field; all the holes and corners; riddling the sty and pigs with Mr. Brown's blunderbuss; bivouacking in the pantry at Victoria's expence; and, when remonstrated with, for mere sport knocking the plaster Albert off the garden wall into the lane. Mr. Latimer de Camp introduces himself more civilly, as Miss Jemima is playing and singing (of course for practice), by accompanying "How happy could I be with either," on the wooden partition with his thumb, after the fashion of a tambarine.

This is the annual busy day.—Packets and parcels are being delivered unceasingly by uncommonly civil butcher-boys, graceful grocers, and urbanic green-grocers, who are near enough to boxing-day to know that silver on the tongue is necessary to charm silver from the pocket. The Captain has sent to learn if any consignments are for him, to ask the loan of a pack of cards, and Victoria's company to spend the evening at the Albert—which invitation is graciously accepted.

CHRISTMAS EVE.
THE FOOD IN PERFECTION.

It is eve—Christmas-eve.—Mrs. Brown's candied mixture, the pudding, is simmering in the copper; the turkey, chine, and hundred etceteras are on their way from Plumpsworth; while Captain de Camp's baggage is at the very wildest verge of that gentleman's imagination, and its appearance would have surprised him more than any one else, so speculative was it.

Mr. Brown is in the City, homeward bound by the omnibus, intending to realize "a Merry Christmas, and a Happy New Year." It is so foggy that he finds he is going at an invisible pace, obliging him to abandon the invisible vehicle in an invisible street, paying an invisible fare.

He ties a handkerchief round his foot to prevent slipping; and has something "short" to keep out the cold; and a little brandy-punch to keep out the fog; and a little egg-flip to keep him warm; and a link that he may see the way, for his vision is not very distinct;— his head is delightfully buoyant, his optics inclined to multiply, and his legs very refractory, having a great desire to dance or go sideways, but obstinately refusing, in their eccentricity, to proceed in a straight line; for Mr. Brown is more merry than particular—taking Newgate Market in his way home to Mizzlington from the 'Change. Having a great veneration for old customs, he buys a boar's head there and boy to carry it; next, being taken with a crockery-shop-sign, "The Little Bason" (which, by-the-bye, was a very large one), he purchases that also, thinking it will do for a wassail-bowl; likewise some holly; and an old butcher's-block to serve as the yule-log; not forgetting the last new Christmas book of sympathy and sentiment, "The Black Beetle on the Hob," a faery tale of a register-

stove, by the author of the "Old Hearth Broom and the Kettle-Holder:"—With these articles Mr. Brown and his retinue reach home in safety—a miracle, considering the toast and ale they have consumed,—the Holly being jolly, the Bason groggy, the Log stupid, and the Boar pig-headed. They find Victoria deaf; for Mr. Brown has made her little gothic door to shiver, and the bolts to chatter with the blows, yet none respond; for the servants are very jovial over boiled ale in the crypt—little thinking or caring about their master; who, after having rung all the bells singly, walked backwards, surveyed the windows, tumbled over the block, and endangered the wassail-bowl, tries ringing all the bells at once without avail; so enters by the back window, and performs a dexterous summerset down the stairs, in company with some evergreens and a flower-stand, ending in a series of double knocks performed upon the inside of the door with the back of his head, and a cuffing from Mr. Brown junior, who happens to be coming in with the key, taking his respected governor for a burglar.

The Browns are next door:—Victoria is fraternizing with Albert, and both are exceedingly happy, although the latter has won greatly at the game of *speculation*—having played his cards well; so, Mr. Brown, after being packed in brown paper, steeped in vinegar, and well soda-watered, joins the social party;—finding Captain de Camp busy concocting an extraordinary oriental mixture (the name of which we quite forget) out of old bottles, from Victoria's cellar; and telling a tremendous Eastern *story* of a tiger captured in a jungle, after a chase of ten hours—he should have said minutes, in a penny magazine!

Mr. Brown and the Captain soon became familiar—in twenty minutes you would have thought them friends of twenty years:—so,—before the last speculator had invested his last weekly sixpence in a goose-club, and drawn the last adamantine old gander; or the last Christmas-pudding-sweep swept away the chimerical puddings, that ought to have been very rich, and everybody thought everybody else had won; before the last trader, who had sold out, dared to mount a notice, intimating that he had joined an "Association to suppress Christmas-boxes,"—the Browns and De Camps had attained that state denominated "thick"—an appellation that might, with propriety, have been applied to Mr. Brown's brains;—for he had obliged Captain de Camp by discounting a bill, due twelve days after date (Christmas), and had invited him to dine on the morrow, to partake of the poultry, that always came up at Christmas, from Plumpsworth; and was taken out in a visit made by the worthy donor, Great-uncle Clayclod, during the "May-meetings," when he does a dozen shilling exhibitions in a day, and knocks up a fly-horse. So, rather late to bed; Mr. Brown making up his Diary, as usual, on the dressing-table—a rule he always observed, though, in some cases, it would have been better left until the morning; for, against December 24th, Tuesday, we find his feelings richly expressed in cramped caligraphy, upside down, bearing evident marks of excitement;—having been penned—in a dream—with hair-dye, mistaken for ink; pounced with carmine, and blotted with the small-tooth-comb in lieu of paper; it is, moreover, curious for its allegorical allusions—likening Captain de Camp to a "brick," a "downey card," a "sharp file," and several other inanimate poetical images.

Of our mild friend, Spohf, he is sleeping soundly upon a light supper—obtained from "St. Stiff's dairy"—some very thin milk, divested of all unctuous quality—that having gone to an epicure Captain, at the Albert Villa. Poor Spohf's talent has not put many talents in his purse—these real racing times run over genius!—they would tunnel Helicon, turn Hippocrene to flush a city's drains,—make Pegasus serve letters by carrying a post-boy, and, in the end, sell the noble beast for feline food:— everything now must be tangible. The little organist, who had spent so many a Merry Christmas with the Browns—he has no pleasure   to   anticipate   on   the

morrow,   "SAFE BIND—SAFE FIND."   except   the performance of his new hymn, "The Star of Bethlehem," a composition of which the little tailor in the attic thought small things, for it did not compose him to sleep.

The 25th of December arrives.—The festival of the year has come. Christmas-day commences with the rising of the cook, who finished the evening, kneading and gaping over pies and puddings; and wakes with the same operation, gaping and kneading her eyes, which do not fairly open until she comes to look after her first care—the pudding:—the fire, having been made up over night, is discovered a "beauty;" but, behold,—within the copper, the pudding has dissolved!—there is nothing to be found but a cloth, which must have been boiling all night in a rich plum-soup,—the string having come untied; or rather, never been tied at all, but popped in by Mrs. B. without attending to that operation:—a piece of neglect, for which the cook gets "warning," and all the servants rated—until the bells of St. Stiff's remind Mrs. B. that it is time to depart, for the duties of a Christian, to eschew all the vanities of this wicked world, in a rich purple Genoa velvet paletot and duck of a plum bonnet. That day Mr. Churchwarden Brown's pue would not hold all, so Mrs. Strap, the pue-opener, had to manœuvre by appropriating part of another to their use, losing her Christmas-box for the offence against its owner, Mr. Din, the copper-smith.

Mr. Spohf's Christmas hymn is much liked, and is really so fine as to make that essence of gentleness, himself, temporarily egotistical; he wonders what impression it has made upon Miss Jemima, and the strange gentleman who is so attentive to her—could he do as much? But Mr. Latimer de Camp is heedless of other good things flying about him; for, upon the walk home after service, among the savoury Christmas dinners that are hurrying in every direction, he is so abstracted as to find a sucking-pig in his stomach, and not a little gravy spilt upon his trowsers, compelling him to change them, upon his arrival at home, for a neat pair of young Brown's.

Good living, at least once a year

Mr. Spohf, having played all out of St. Stiff the Martyr, walks home moodily:—instead of finding his dinner as usual, the chop and potato, he learns that his landlord, Mr. Strap, the greengrocer, has stopped the supplies. It is quarter-day!—Strap thinks of the five weeks' arrears, and Mr. Spohf's inability to pay for his lodgings; so, Mr. and Mrs. Strap have surprised him, by preparing a huge leg of mutton and pudding; for they know he does not, as of old, go to the "Willer." After this humble repast, which was relished as much as any could be, and was far less likely to leave unpleasant sensations than if it had been more costly, they draw round the fire; and master Ichabod Strap, one of the choristers of St. Stiff the Martyr, is playing with a shilling, polishing the coin upon his sleeve—it is the identical one said to have been put in the plate by Captain de Camp, and given by Mr. Flyntflayer (the gentleman who held the gothic platter) to Mrs. Strap, the pue-opener, advising her at the same time to nail it to the counter—a counterfeit to deter "smashers." But, somehow, the coin seemed doomed to remain unholy, for no orifice or artifice could have rendered it a *lucky* one; it was shown to Mr. Spohf, who thought it bad, and that it might have gotten into the plate by mistake; Mrs. Strap knew it bad—an intentional perpetration,—and, like the giver, not worth a dump; Mr. Strap not only thought it bad, but proved it so; for, after having spun, sounded, and eaten a portion of it, he cast the coin into the glowing fire, where the silver quickly changed, dropping, like quick-silver, among the ashes, to be picked out by Ichabod, very unlike a sterling coin.

Old Strap, who had taken "the pledge," but since introduced an exceptional clause in favour of feasts and

festivals,

gets out the black bottle for fraternity's sake. They take a pipe a-piece, and so softened is the little organist with their genuine unsophisticated kindness, that he sees all his cares fly, and nothing but joys in the wreathed curls of smoke betaking themselves up the chimney:—he sees Messrs. Blow and Grumble, the eminent organ-builders, making a fortune by his "new movement;" having purchased and patented it: he has found a publisher for his church music, and sold his old opera. Captain de Camp has vanished in smoke—he has exploded of spontaneous combustion,—they find him all deceit, leaving a glass eye and a cork leg. Mr. Latimer gets the Colonial Bishopric of Bushantee, in New Zealand, and cuts Miss Jemima. Mr. Wellesley having gone to India for glory, returns with it,—a hook, and a patch over his eye. Miss Angelina vows to die a virgin. Mr. Brown says to Mr. Spohf, "my son!"—Mr. Spohf says to Mr. Brown, "my father!" Mr. Strap is standing in triumph upon a pyramid of "carpets to beat," viewing a lesser one of "boots to brush;" having been entrusted with more "messages" than mortal ever could "deliver;" whilst innumerable vans, bearing the name of Strap, traverse innumerable roads in "Town and Country." Mrs. Strap, dressed in a plain plum silk, turns a mahogany mangle, and gets up nothing but "fine things." Ichabod has cut the choir, and made his *début* in an opera as Herr Strapii, a perfect triumph.

But here we will leave Mr. Spohf's reverie—for Victoria and reality; where the company is arriving to the annual dinner, and sitting about the drawing-room, looking as happy as patients at a dentist's; or festive, as disappointed toadeaters at the funeral of an opulent relative, who had left all his property to found an asylum for decayed postboys—after leading everybody to expect the lion's share of it:—the guests, for want of more exciting topics, admiring the gimcracks they admired a year ago; thinking the portrait of Mr. Brown—"done," twenty years since, at a portrait club,— a splendid likeness, and that the original grows younger (query, richer?); stating truths and untruths about the weather; inquiring energetically after each other's health—not caring for

27

the answers; with other homely pleasantries, too numerous to mention; until some of the juveniles—the only ones who really seem at home—espy from the window a loaded parcel-cart; this they observe as funny on a Sunday (little thinking, at that moment, it was Tuesday). Here Mr. Brown descends, to hold an altercation with the guard of that cart, who makes light of a huge hamper of game; whilst the guests at the windows above, speculate upon having to eat an uncooked turkey, or fancy their ravenous appetites waiting while it is cooked—the youngsters calculating upon a dinner all pudding. Mr. Brown returns, and tenders his arm to Lady Lucretia de Camp—in the excitement, leading her down the side where the stairs taper to nothing,—causing that lady to lose both equilibrium and temper.

THE PUDDING.
AS IT OUGHT TO HAVE APPEARED.

In the hall they are introduced to the viands, all thought to partake of;—which have arrived too late, and are now displayed in their primitive state—a picture of still life; whilst the guests—a picture of disappointment—have to put up with odds and ends, concocted to meet the emergency, ending with a series of plum-dumplings, in place of the legitimate large pudding. However, the indigent relatives, who prefer the cold corners, and take "any part," declare themselves well satisfied:—all partaking of everything, and brandy afterwards, as if the viands were rich. Master Brown does justice to everything, of course—that sweet child is now pulling the *merry thought* with his maiden aunt; he is victor, and, as no one wishes to know his *thoughts*, seems determined to tell them,—wishing "Jemy. and Mr. Latimer would look sharp, and knock up the match Mamma spoke of; as then he should be breeched, have pockets, and money:" here the little dear turned to the Captain, saying, "You'll give me a crown, won't you?"—a question at which the maiden aunt blushed intensely, as did Mrs. Brown, who attempted to hide her emotion by saying, "What strange things children do think of!"—at the same time helping a gentleman who had had enough—the bashful gentleman, who sat at the junction of the tables, and appeared so incommoded by the table-land of one being higher than the table-land of the other—causing his plate to oscillate in a very remarkable manner, and discharge its contents in his lap,—the conjoined legs compelling him either to sit at a fearful distance, and spill the gravy, or to split his kerseymeres, by extending them too much for their frail make:—however, he has at last succeeded in thrusting one knee between them, and the shorter leg of the two off Bunyan's "Pilgrim's Progress"—used to stilt it;—letting the unfortunate gentleman's pudding down, and his plate travel, until at last it stops, performing a gyration, all to itself, under the sideboard.

The Merry Thought

During this clatter, the ladies rise and depart, leaving the gentlemen to drown all disappointments in the wine. Mr. Brown, "feeling called upon," rises, apologizing for certain misfortunes, herein described—at the same time trusting that such events might never happen again; and, in the end, eulogizing Mrs. B., who is painted in glowing colours, by a painter who said he should not have painted it; or, as any one else might have observed, introduced two virtuously amiable daughters, so prominently in the foreground. After a noble reply by Captain de Camp, of the Hon. East India Company's service, from Madras, and much applause from the diners, they ascend, to join the ladies; forming, round the drawing-room-fire, a vast amphitheatre, in the centre of which, gladiatorial children contend for nuts and oranges—

Captain de Camp filling the post of honour,—making himself at home in Mr. Brown's easy chair and slippers. Mr. Wellesley drags in the yule-log, much to the detriment of the Brussels, and the annoyance of the guests; for, upon placing it in the grate, it causes everything to be covered with black tadpoles, nearly extinguishing the fire—until it ignites, roasting the company, and making the pot a white-heat.

The Captain has repeated last evening's brew, upon a larger scale, in the "little bason," or wassail-bowl. Master Wellesley has kissed Angelina under the mistletoe, suspended from the chandelier, and placed in the centre of the amphitheatre, for that purpose. Mr. Latimer has "taken the opportunity," as Jemima turned up a refractory burner; and everybody kissed everybody else they liked, or could catch there. The entertaining Captain has narrated an effective anecdote of an enraged elephant, and a precious big boar speared in a savage jungle—to which he might have added, with no more personal risk than Mrs. Brown may experience when hunting for a boa in her wardrobe. And, Mr. Mouldy, the city merchant, who dealt in rags, sang about a little excitable pig, and "Mac Mullin's Lament;" whilst Mr. Snobbins—who it was hoped would sit and be silent,—has broken the spell, dared to remember old times, sleeping under a counter, and the pugnacity of Brown, when they were in a mess at the *blues*—making Captain de Camp think more of a military repast than Christ's Hospital;—until the "*blues*" were dispelled by Mr. Snobbins singing "The gallant 'prentice boy:"—not that the company would have lacked a military man, had the Captain been absent, for there was Cowed, the meek Bermondsey tanner, by livery a hatter, and withal a soldier—a member of the Hon. Artillery Company,—he who sang about God blessing the old cow's hide, and a

"Wish that his soul in heaven might dwell,

Who first invented the leather bottel;"

—and, Mrs. Brown's brother, Mr. Barthe Brick, familiarly known as the "Brick," who had just commenced a song, a parody upon Fra Diavolo,—a something very, very low, supposed to be sung by a dealer in hearth-stones; who, at the end of each verse, vociferates "who'll buy," heightening the illusion by trundling a chair, on its back, round the family circle, to represent a barrow.

No one knows where the barbarous atrocities would have ended, and all before the refined strangers, too, had not the olive-branches—disposed for rest by their several mammas in the room above—all awoke at once, tumbled out of bed, and joined in a combined cry; this breaks the family circle—mothers fly to pack their turbulent innocents for travel; the candles flare, and carriages clatter, grinding the flints in the lane. John, the footman, finds he has a dozen half-crowns, and Mary seven. The last fly has departed with the little Bricks; lights appear and disappear in the bed-chambers; and the Christmas-day—that comes but once a year—has vanished, like a dream!

Mr. Brown has jotted the events, in his Diary, in a hand scarcely legible. It must have been penned in a somnambulistic fit—thinking he was at a meeting of St. Stiff's vestry, in the union board-room,—for, after a list of member's present (the names of his guests), Captain de Camp in the chair, follow these minutes of proceedings:—Firstly, that one Spohf be dismissed as organist of St. Stiff's, confined in the idiot-ward, fed on water gruel, and handed over to his own parish (Vienna); proposed by Latimer, and seconded by Wellesley de Camp. The second proposition appears to be to the effect that a vagrant named Brick, dealer in hearth-stones, be confined in the refractory-ward, and fed upon bread and water.

The morning after the festivities London oversleeps itself:—and, awaking, finds it boxing-day. Variegated dips are being disseminated among delighted, dirty, juveniles; whilst the boys seem chagrined at notices for "the extinction of abuses," or "suppression of Christmas-boxes;" which seems only to make them the more pertinacious at Victoria Villa: for an irregular dustman has chalked the post, and the Postman vowed to mark Mr. Brown; the Turncock is turned off; the Waits have to "wait a little longer;" and the Beadle, who declared Mr. Brown no generous

churchwarden, has, withal, found enough alcohol to make him stupid before night—causing that dignitary to cry a lost boy instead of a girl, and to see twice as many posts round St. Stiff's as usual; taking half of them to be boys about to vault over the other half, he rushes on to disperse them, soundly chastising the granite.

All the little boys secure their mites before mid-day; taking their posts at the gallery-door of a popular theatre, five hours before opening, to practise that rare virtue, patience, at the shrine of "Hot Codlings," and "George Barnwell."

Master Ichabod Strap, in his richest yellow breeches, and burnished badge of St. Stiff the Martyr, is perambulating the parish with his gay phylactery, or Christmas-piece—"The History of Joseph," painted, like the coat, in many colours:—he shows it to Mrs. Brown, who approves the performance; "stroking the head of modest and ingenuous worth that blushed at its own praise;" measuring the boy at a glance, and proffering him promotion in the shape of an uniform, of buttons, just vacated by a youth—called by his peers "Nobby Jones," but by his mistress "Alphonso;"—who, having grown to the great risk of buttons and stitches, was dispossessed of his regimentals, being sent home one dark night in his bed-gown. "Ichabod" promises to resign that title and all connection with the dirty boys, to reign as Alphonso the second page; being missed by Mr. Spohf, for whom he used to blow the organ, in the little second floor—a bereavement Mrs. B. enjoyed, saying, she wondered how the unworthy little animal would raise the wind now.

BOXING DAY.

AN OFFENDED DIGNITARY OF THE CHURCH.
'BOLISH THE BOXES, INDEED, 'SPECT NEXT THEY'L 'BOLISH THE
BISHOPS.—WHAT'S A SEASON WITHOUT COMPLIMENTS!

There is an universal adage about risking sprats to capture
herrings—a sport not unknown to our cosmopolite Captain, for he
had fished in troubled waters, and hunted for a dinner many a
time;—he knew the traps and snares to secure game, the days and
seasons; so, on Boxing-day, he baits the servants with crowns;

Tommy with a sovereign; Angelina with "The Keepsake;" Jemima with a modern-ancient missal, or portion of Scripture made dear and difficult to read; presenting Mrs. B. with the last new art manufacture—"The Knowing Blade, a brazen-faced sharper, to remove blunt;" and procuring for Mr. B. the skin of the identical Bengal tiger he killed, as may be seen from a legend running up the back bone—though an inscription on the tip of the tail states it to be sold by Fitch of Regent Street. The bait secures its amount of flat-fish; for that evening, Captain de Camp was more than usually lucky—he caught enough at ecarté to clear himself;—a freak of fortune that caused no asperity in the noble breast of Brown; for here are his own thoughts in his own words:— "December 26th, Wednesday (Boxing-day).—My dear friend, De Camp, has this day given us all tokens of the warmest attachment—sadly wanting to do something for me—'Colonial,' 'War,' or 'Admiralty.' Not requiring anything just now, this will form an admirable reserve; I must, in the meantime, profit by his refined society, as I hope and trust the girls will by his sons'. If there be any drawback to the delight I feel, it is the non-arrival of his luggage; for I am personally inconvenienced by his wearing my best coat. I may be over-scrupulous in wishing he would return the books he devours with such avidity:—Mrs. B. says, she thinks, the paragon of knowledge swallows them; for they are not to be found."

Next morning Ichabod enters the Brown suit and service, having spent Boxing-night and the proceeds of the Christmas-piece at the play, where he saw "Jane Shore" and "Harlequin House that Jack built;" the plot and tricks of which he recounted to Master Tommy, as he took that young gentleman for a walk, inoculating him with a great desire to go and behold it. So, after having coaxed his mother, teased his father, and cried his lovely blue eyes into a good imitation of red veined marble, the youth triumphed; for on Thursday evening, they all went to the play in the fusty fly from Drone's yard, driven by old Drone, in his pepper-and-salt suit of pseudo livery, that looked as if he always brushed it with the currycomb; and so tindery about the breast, fromthe number of marriage-favours annually pinned there, that it is a wonder it holds together. Alphonso rode upon the box, giving the vehicle a certain amount of smartness. On their arrival under the dirt-embrowned portico of the theatre, they are cordially recognised by the De Camps; who, thinking it a pity the box should not be filled, have just dropped down to see "London Assurance"—intending to quit before the pantomime, but forgetting to do so after all.

During the play, Master Tommy disposes of a vast quantity of oranges and sponge-cakes—vanishing between each act to obtain a fresh supply;—making butterflies of the bill, and causing the double-barrelled *lorgnette* (which was hired for the occasion from an adjacent oyster-shop) to slip off the cushion, falling upon a bald gentleman in the pit:—the excited little pest remarking everything, and fairly shouting at the discovery of Alphonso below, until chid by his mother. Oh! that we could participate in thy youthful enthusiasm, or feel pleased at that hotch-potch—the overture; or, a thrill when the muffin-bell tinkles, causing the lovely drop-scene—that combined the grandeur of the pretty Parthenon with the sublimity of Virginia Water—to vanish into its own intensely blue sky; disclosing the "Harlequin House that

Jack built," and Mr. John Bull's huge paste-board thick head, snoring like thunder, in a "property" summer-house—an elephantine blue-bottle on his proboscis, and a sleeping bull-dog, the size of an Alderney steer, at his feet:—here Master Brown, with a grin, calls the house Victoria Villa, and the paste-board mask his papa. Now enters the rat, to eat the good things that lay in the house that John built, represented by a stealthy seedy gentleman, who, after reading a board intimating that apartments were to let, crept slyly past the sleepy Bull, to mount the house-steps; and there deliver himself of the following doggerel, in a mellifluous voice:—

"I search for lodgings—here's the very thing,—

Though I've not got a *rap*, I think I'll *ring*;

For all I want is to be *taken in*,—

As I would others *take*—sure 'tis no sin

To do to others—only tit for tat—

So here goes—Rat—tat, tat—a tat!!!!!"

The orchestra, loud in wishing to know "who's dat knocking at de door?" and Master Tom, deep in the bill, with Mr. Rat, who is there described as a "scamp"—an unknown term to Tom, for he asked its meaning; observing that Uncle Brick said Captain de Camp was a scamp. This question remained unanswered; for no one heard it except the Captain, who felt a great itching to pull a young monkey's ears, but did not. The cat (a sort of Puss in Boots, with a short stick and strip of paper) entering, to catch the rat, is worried by the dog; who is tossed by a cow with a very crumpled horn; who was milked by a maid said to be very forlorn; who is kissed by a sweet-looking beggar, all tattered and torn— the loving pair being likened to Jemima and Latimer, by Master Tom, causing his sister's face to redden as a furnace, that heightened the more it was fanned; and when the priest, all shaven and shorn (whom Tom called the Rev. Loyalla à Becket), commenced marrying the couple, then Miss Jemima entertained serious notions of fainting; and, probably, would, had not the solemnization of matrimony been violated by the priest, who shed his sack-cloth surplice, vaulting over the rails of the altar, between the astonished couple, leaving that sanctuary to change into a *match maker's*—appearing, himself, a perfect *clown*, stating that sublime, veritable, truth—*"here we are again!"*—working his geometric, chromatic, physiognomy into endless contortions, extending his arms like the sails of contrary windmills, twiddling his legs like a fly,—and when called upon, by unearthly voices, for "Tippytiwitchet," appears so scared that he tumbles through the big drum, to oblige them with the song from the slips; instantly afterwards presenting himself upon the stage, dilating his spotted inexpressibles, until they put him in mind of a friend, *Pantaloon*, that, by a curious coincidence, resides at a tailor's, in the back-ground, having just completed a patch-work skin, for *Harlequin*; who, the instant he is fitted, flies through the panel of a door, inscribed *"cutting-out room,"* into the next house, a *florist's*, there to obtain his favourite flower, the *Columbine*, with whom he has a long dance in the centre of a very solitary street; whilst Clown and Pantaloon arrange a partnership concern, which they carry on in the middle of the road, in front of the shop, until Clown renders himself more plague than profit, by warming his partner's lumbar region with a very red-hot goose, basting him with the sleeve-board, and sticking him to the road with wax— Clown dissolving partnership by walking off, in a new wrap-rascal, with the cash-box, that no one may rob them. The best things must come to an end!—and so does the Pantomime—with a gorgeous display of red fire, tinsel and gold, real water and the electric light—all chopped off in the middle by the descending curtain. The box-fronts have been enveloped in their night-gowns; the   Columbine   is   clattering,   in   pattens, to   her

THE NOTORIOUS SINGER AT THE "WALRUS," SINGING HIS
CELEBRATED DITY "THE DROP" AND "THE DRAIN."

lodgings; the Harlequin has been bolted out, unable to vault through the fan-light; and the Clown is running in his painted face, having

44

forgotten to wash it, for at home he left a dear wife seriously ill, to come and be funny in sadness.

Drone's fly is homeward bound, heavily laden. The young men of the party have dived into "The Welsh Rarebit Warren," there to spend the early hours of the morning, listening to sentimental songs chanted amid fumes of tobacco and spirits, to hear sorry wit, and make vapid remarks. The great feature of the evening being a melodramatic dirge, supposed to be sung by a condemned felon—a triumphant lamentation and delineation of brutal character,—so eloquent and thrilling, in its monosyllabic groans of anguish, that it is a wonder the kidneys, consumed in such numbers, are ever digested. But, alas!—such is life—those most swayed by animal propensities see the least warning therein:—as, the thief combines business and pleasure at the gallow's foot; so, with the frequenters of the "Warren"—they imbue their sentiment and supper,—only digesting the latter. Wellesley has devoured several "rabbits," and Latimer disposed of numberless kidneys, whilst young Brown has had to wait the usual forty minutes for a steak; and, in the interim, had five "stouts," four "goes," and several cigars, i.e., with assistance from the De Camps; who have made free, ay, to order goblets of champagne, and, in the end, not having change to repair the "damage" (a mean, but true, term, as often applied), they get young Brown to pay the complicated sum added up by the waiter, upon a mahogany ditto, in lieu of a slate, with stale stout spilled in the corner, receipted with a wipe of the towel:—and so, home in the "safety" cab, with large wheels and a spanking grey,—lettered along the side "*Nil desperandum,*" thinking "handsome is as *Hansom* does;" tumbling into bed just before the peep o' day, and five hours after Mr. Brown had made up his Diary—writing against December the 27th., Thursday, that he had taken Tom and the girls to a pantomime; been agreeably surprised to find the De Camps there, especially the sons, who did sit in front, with Jemy. and Angel., looking made as much for one another as he could desire:—Tom behaving very sadly; and, were it not for his mother, the boy should spend the vacations at a Yorkshire school;—twice every year—in the Dog-days and December—is the house turned topsy-turvy,—it may be sport to you, Master Tom, but 'tis death to us.

Thus older grew the year, and fuller got the Diary—Mr. Brown graphically recounting the doings and disasters of "December 28th, Friday.—Unpropitious, fatal, Friday! I never knew it lucky save once, and then it *was*—I let the Albert. 'Christmas comes but once a year,' with a train of nasty bills, not to be bilk'd; and sorry consolation is it thinking you 'paid at the time,' when the receipt is not to be found. Miss-Fortune, that never came single, now visits with a large family of little pests—out of season and uninvited!—Here is Needy, the pianist, who, one would think, had married her; for he has children enough to fill a charity school. Needy, of No. 9, Brown Terrace, has absconded without paying the rent—sending the key, and £12. 10s., instead of £14., with a shabby excuse about hoping to be able to make up the difference some day:—this is the return for showing compassion to a poor devil!—I ought to have known, when I took the cottage-piano for last quarter, though Spohf did say it was a six-and-three-quarters, worth three times the money!—I am a good-natured fool, and ought, in justice to my family, to be a little more selfish—these mean professionals estimating their rubbish far beyond all reason!—My spirits are damped—and so are we all, for the water-pipes that that rascal Plummer fixed, at the low contract, have burst with this evening's thaw, and were discovered just as the water was coming in; having played, I know not how long, a fountain in the bathroom, tumbling down the stairs like the falls of the Niagara, obliging us to insert tobacco-pipes all over the drawing-room ceiling, to drain the 39inundation:—it has spoilt the watered paper, stained the aquatint of the Aqueduct, and 'Wellington at Waterloo,' done for the water-gilding, and saturated the 'Momentous Question;' the 'Heart's Misgivings' is a sop; and the water-colour of the 'Flood' is washed away. Alphonso is sitting up in goloshes to empty the pots, and I doubt much if I shall sleep over the dropping-well."

How Mr. Brown slept we do not know, but can imagine, for here is the Diurnal Record, made up in bed:— "December 29th, Saturday.—Dreamed Victoria Villa turned into a hydropathic establishment—that I was being frozen, thawed, and suffocated; did wake, this day, with an enlarged cheek—the influenza compelling me to keep my bed, bathe my chilblains, and anoint my nose; I take slops internally, and wear a heart upon the outside of my chest. The kind, considerate Captain called, smoking a cigar, that made me cough, and think his visit a visitation."

COMPLIMENTS OF THE SEASON.

The first Sunday after Christmas is here:—Brown is in bed; the little bell of St. Stiff's has stopped, and many another vibratory sound is dying in the distance; flakes of snow are moodily descending—causing the fire to spit angrily, and the face of heaven to look black—all light appearing to come from the earth;

sound is deadened, the carpet is darker than usual, and the ceiling lighter; Mr. Brown's eyes are up there, for he is lying, tracing amid the cracks and stains, vast palaces like pictures by Martin, or aërial phantasmagorias by Turner. Brown is lying, nursing his influenza according to the approved adage; though 40some read the maxim thus, "Stuff a cold, and (have to) starve a fever." Let us hope Brown has the right version. Captain de Camp has come to read to the invalid, and drink his brandy and water—he has begun "Blair's Sermons," or rather the life of Blair, prefixed to the volume, in a full conviction of its religious tendency; whilst in the room above is John, the footman, standing upon his bed, breathing on the single pane of glass, inserted in the sloped roof, that he may melt the snow, and see to read a mysterious document—a tumbled note,—not on the Bank of England, but an epistolatory one, found in the trowsers pockets of Mr. Latimer de Camp—the same cast off by that gentleman on Christmas-day, when he stumbled over the strange dinner, in coming from church, and so much deteriorated their appearance as to give them to John;—who now, thinking he has found evidence,—thinks he always thought he thought the De Camps scamps. John is perplexed at the purport of the letter; and feeling a cold thrill run through him, he turns into bed, there to reflect for ten minutes upon the downy pillow, pondering with intensely closed eyes, considering before he puts himself in the power of an enemy—for John had been a soldier once, and would have been one now, had not his poor old mother starved and mangled together enough to buy him off; he bore the stamp of military drill, took in "Tales of the Wars," in penny numbers, and had a cheap print of the "Battle of Waterloo" pasted to the sloping roof, above the bed, in which we left him pondering. Having considered enough, he takes once more to the document, folding and unfolding it, examining the thimble impress on the seal, tasting a corner of it in his excitement, and reading it with intense energy for the last time: it is directed to "Latimer de Camp, Esq., M.A., Albert Villa, Mizzlington;" and was posted in the New Cut:—

No. 2, Grubb's Rents.

"Dear Edward,

"I am anxiously awaiting the 'Conspiracy,'—do not keep me in suspense!—do DO it, for my benefit.—I sadly want money. Is the plot too horrible for you!—you know how to do for a 'Victoria' company!—make a domestic tragedy of it—shoot the father and son!—you know the rest. Pray communicate, or I shall think you in trouble.

"Your forlorn—Emma."

For this last perusal John appears none the wiser, being unable to divine more than at first—murder and treachery seem the plot. John thinks the Captain just like Gory, the murderer, in the Chamber of Horrors, at the wax-works; and that Victoria Villa resembles "Greenacre Hall," depicted in the pictorial newspaper. John is sadly perplexed as to where he shall seek counsel—of course, thinking of every one foreign to the case; until, happily, he remembers one that ought to have been thought of first—to Mr. Spohf will he send the mysterious note, ask his advice, and act upon it:—but, unfortunately, John sealed the envelope with Mr. Brown's crest—a circumstance that made Mr. Spohf think the letter from his old friend Brown; so he answers it as such—feeling much pleasure that *his* advice should be sought;—saying, the enclosed note appeared to be about some drama some one had to write—a document of no serious import. As to *strangers*, he should advise caution; for it is the aim of a rogue to look as much like a trusty friend as possible; quiet watchfulness is well, for that can harm no one. This answer from Mr. Spohf was promptly delivered by the little tailor's daughter to the expectant John; who naturally thought it for him. Curiously, John and his master both owned the name of Brown—John Brown:—now John, the servant, was conscientious; and would not, on any account, have opened his master's letters—he drew the line of propriety much further off,—it stopped at reading in at the ends. John felt sure *this* letter was for him—not that he liked being called an esquire; yet, for all that, he felt safe, for there, extra-large and important, was the word *"Private"*—a military distinction that made him doubly certain; so, he bore away the letter, in great trepidation, to his quarters in the tiles, there to be much relieved by its contents; vowing, as he lay on his bed, to be watchful as the Duke on the look-out in his "Battle of Waterloo," and dumb as a dead drummer in the foreground.

Happily Victoria and Albert were ignorant of these despatches, or John might have lost his commission and uniform. Confidence is unshaken;—for, on December 30th, *Sunday*, Captain de Camp is reported a "glorious oriental brick,"—he having kindly prescribed all sorts of good things for his invalid friend, without the slightest regard to expense; and, moreover, broken Brown's quinsy by administering an extraordinary anecdote, or "crammer," that scarcely any one could *swallow*; but Brown did, and laughed so much afterwards, that the quinsy was gone; for the Captain had anecdotes suited to all times and seasons—he only wanted listeners, and off he went like an alarum. Sunday put him in mind of that day twelvemonths; and that day put him in mind of Richard Spark, of the Native Infantry; Rich. Spark put him in mind of how they got that Hindoo millionaire, Makemuchjee Catch-muchjee, into a Christian church, by walking him between them, in a state of ether; how he (the Hindoo) was mollified by the sermon, and went home—melted the Idol, Boobobum, that had golden hair, diamond eyes, pearly teeth, coral lips, a silver tongue, and a copper bottom; how he handed her over in lumps to the church; and yet, with all these poetical attributes she was the ugliest and most precious god he ever set eyes on. She was the subscription of the district—the poor put the copper and the rich the gold;—the Captain telling of how he made a posthumous portrait of her, which is quite correct; only he forgot five bosoms in the bust, and left out a right arm:—it is engraved in No. 365 of the "Missionary Record."

This paragraph opens with the last day of the old year.—The cold that stiffened Mr. Brown's neck, and choked up his throat has thawed; his nose has resumed its accustomed hue; his temper is unusually good in the prospect of vacating his room, and beginning the year with redoubled energy. Mrs. Brown is preparing for something important; and, from the delicate scented note you observed inserted in our chimney-glass-frame—the one with the Brown crest, a rampant locomotive proper, and motto of "Go-a-head" (which, between ourselves, was *found* by a very subtle seal-engraver in Change Alley);—from that, and the remarks of Master Brown, when we called this morning, you may pretty well judge:—he said Jemy. wrote such a lot o' letters the other day; that they have a pillow-case filled with oranges—quite a sack-full; and, moreover, his Ma'. just was clever—for she said she could kill two parties with one chandelier, and make rout-seats hold double! The fact is, Mrs. Brown intends to give a ball on the 4th of January, and a juvenile party on the 5th—the former to be extra-superb, on account of the De Camps; who, of course, are expected—having received an invitation by post. We wonder the Browns did not write to invite themselves; for John passed the Albert door in taking the Captain's letter to the post, and the preparations were as much under the guidance of those worthies as of the Browns themselves. The boudoir is in a litter—all cuttings of satin and book muslin,—in the midst of which may be seen pretty Miss Bib and little Madame Tucker, very busily employed—Lady Lucretia de Camp proffering advice; and superintending the construction of an amber satin, covered with black lace—a dress that Mrs. Brown thought to wear, but felt obliged to resign, so much did her kind patron, Lady de Camp, dote upon it.

Above this last-named apartment is Brown's bedchamber, where he and the Captain are spending a quiet evening, reviewing their prospects and relating their experiences:—the Captain stating his intention of living retired upon his property, for all his friend Major Cant's trying to persuade him to take an adjoining house in Belgravia. No! he was content to stay where he was—Albert was snug; but if Mr. Brown thought of removing to Mayfair or Tyburnia, why then, a house next such a capital individual might be a desideratum:—he said it—an Army Captain that should not say it, but did not care,—stock-brokers and merchants were men of bottom; though probably his friend Major Cant would say *that* bottom meant the *baser* stuff they were composed of—the joke was better than the simile, and neither bad. After this opinion the Captain paused to think, drink, and—with a blow that made the table quiver,—demand, to know what a man without money was *worth?*—answering the question, in the same breath, with an emphatic *nothing!*—a man of wealth *was* a man of worth! We know not if Mr. Brown thought this logic or no;—but he, Captain de Camp, knew it, and intended to let his friends know it also; for next season he would give a grand entertainment, get Spread and Co. to throw a marquee over the lawn, and see if Major Cant would come—the Captain rather thought *he*would; or the Hon. Sam. Dummy—the coxcomb, who, when asked to dine with Alderman Fig, in Bloomsbury Square, said *his*horses never crossed Tottenham Court Road—Stinkomalee and the Brutish Museum savouring too much of the "people" for the exquisite;—but the Captain winked, and said he knew how the Dummy would get out of the fix—he would come along the New Road, as the Captain said he once knew him do, when in search of an asthmatic poodle that had been stolen, and was at a dog-fancier's on Pentonville Hill. Then should we have the lane filled with carriages, like at a Chiswick fête; I would introduce my friend to the world, and be at rest;—for we are a couple of old boys, willing to make sacrifices for our dear children.

Having delivered himself of these lofty sentiments as the bells were ringing out the old year—stopping to strike its knell;—the

Captain also stopped, to seize a glass and the hand of Brown—wishing him the merriest, maniest, and happiest of New Years;—drinking eternal unity to the B.'s and De C.'s—at the same time shedding a very visible tear, that dropped into his brandy and water, like the pearl of Cleopatra, to be sacrificed to self—to a very affectionate man—so *very* affectionate, that he loved himself, we do believe.

The spirits and sentiment so overcame Brown, that he buried his emotion in the bolster—a state of mind the Captain did not fail to observe, and take advantage of; for—"he supposed Mr. Brown could *not* spare £8, until Saturday?"—An affirmation that gentleman repudiated; for he granted the small favour with pleasure—presenting the leaf of an oblong book, and his autograph, to the Captain; who retired with the same—by an ingenious plan to render it of ten times the value—adding to the *eight* a letter *y*, making it eighty, and the figure to keep company with a naught—£80.

The events of this day are chronicled in the Diary of Brown—all *couleur de rose*,—the literal purport of which it would be tedious to repeat; suffice it to say, the aphorisms on the demise of the year ran foul of the "*occasional memoranda*," and were brought to a dead stop by the "*general accounts*;" not that his ideas stopped on paper, for he continued them in bed. Brown dreamed "his ship had come home;"—that he dwelt in a Belgravian palace; that he was an M.P.;—that he was known as *Brown*, the "King of 'Change"—that he ruled with an iron ruler—that he was enthroned upon a cash-box—that he wore a crown of dollars—that the four quarters of the globe adored him—that Great and Little Britain worshipped him;—that the *world* told his *wife*, Brown was a great man:—but, alas!—trains of wild ideas, like locomotives that go too fast, may run off the rail when least expected, or explode as a train of gunpowder, without notice; so, in Mr. Brown's imagination, he feels as if shot into the air, after being dreadfully scalded—Mrs. Brown, kind soul, having applied a bottle of boiling water (forgetting the flannel) to the feet of her spouse, before retiring, herself—that good lady little thinking it was so warm. But there were other things Mrs. Brown did not know of; for she little thought the servants were round the kitchen-fire, quiet as mice, all deep in the "Mysteries of the Courts and Sewers of London"— a work affording the greatest amount of horrible excitement at the lowest rate,—a book in which Alphonso has discovered a Captain de Camp; and cook, a Lady Thingamy, whom, she says, "ain't no better than she should be"—a rather vague but significant truth, that might as appropriately have been applied to a saint as to a sinner, though cook intended it for the latter:—as to the Capting, the only think she had agin him was a wish he wouldn't spile everythink with soy and cayenne, for it got into the wash, and made the pigs sneeze. Mary, too, must have her opinion— saying Wellesley wasn't no gentleman, for he wiped his dirty boots on the towels, and would pull the plug out of the wash-bason when there was nothing under to catch the soapy water. During this scandal, John, whom all thought knew something, only said the Captain was *an umbug*—as he noiselessly disappeared, bearing his shoes in his hand; for it was considerably past midnight.

Young Brown and his two friends are at the "Planets" harmonic meeting, stating their intention not to return till morning—an useless proclamation, for it is impossible to do otherwise, now—they having been at the Casino, "getting their feet in," for the hop on Friday, as young Brown termed the practice of dancing.

Mr. Spohf is in bed, but cannot sleep—so great is his pleasure,—Messrs. Blow and Grumble having patented "Spohf's new organ-movement."

"A Happy New Year—and may you live to see many of them!"—The New Year is born with every characteristic of its defunct sire—seeming no better behaved (as some people would have little boys after a birthday or a breeching):—the old year died with a drizzle; and the young one, that everybody hoped promising, is born with the same attributes.

Mr. Brown is at his post again—the parish lamp-post at the corner of the lane—awaiting the "Favourite" omnibus, that is to bear him to the City. He is trying to arrange the thousand and one little commissions he has to execute for Mrs. Brown. How many he remembered or forgot we know not; but that day he purchased a fair blank Diary—the stationer who sold it not only wishing him "a Happy New Year," but that he might "live to fill fifty such:"—a wish that made Mr. Brown very contemplative—thinking 18,250 entries no joke;—of many bright, bright days of pleasure; two score and ten of birthdays; half a century of weddings, anniversaries, and deaths—let us hope of peaceful, happy deaths,—for clouds will sometimes gather, darkening the brightest sky; but, thank Heaven, there is plenty of sunshine for those who seek it—ay, to find it, too, though it be midnight and beside a kitchen-fire. Of this new Diary the first page is penned with more care than usual—as all first pages are:—there the De Camp dynasty reign in confidence; and it is evident that Mr. Brown anticipates a glorious future.

Young Time, we have often imagined, must be born fledged; for he can fly quickly as his sire!—It is the 3rd of January—the day prior to Mrs. Brown's ball.—Thus thought we, wending our way to Victoria Villa; having promised the Miss Browns to step in and practise the "*deux-temps*" with them; but, as we have since heard, it is another new double-shuffle that is turning the brains of the dancing world just now;—however, we went, and found Victoria in a pretty pickle—a perfect mixed pickle, we may say,—our dear young friends being so much too busy to remember the appointment:—for there was the "Broadwood" standing upon the landing; and Master Tom cutting out slides upon the bare boards in the drawing-room, the carpet being taken to St. Stiff's Union, that it might be beaten—a thing we exceedingly rejoiced in; for last year the guests were obliged to beat it with their feet, and afterwards to carry the dust home upon their shoulders—the first polka being performed as if in the Great Desert, during a sand-storm. There was the chandelier (that looked all the year like a giant pear enveloped in holland) being removed to the parlour, and a much more splendid one suspended in its stead. We peeped into the drawing-room, and had our dignity compromised by a man on some steps; who directed us to "look alive and bring that hammer." So, it being very evident we were in the way, we withdrew, tumbling over a barricade of fenders and other furniture in the hall, raised during our absence by the insurgent housemaids; who, we are sorry to say, seemed rather diverted at the mishap, for we heard them giggle, though of course we appeared not to notice, and tried to walk away with a joyous air; at the same time vowing never to visit, even our best friends, on the day prior to a party.

So we took care to keep away until the memorable evening arrived; but being particularly requested to come early, and bring our amiable sisters, we wished to do so. The Brougham was waiting, as were we—thinking to do so for some time:—having made up our mind and the study-fire—diving deep into the first book handy—an "Essay upon Light and Shade in Painting." Well, we were in the dark—with Rembrandt;—when the room appeared to fill with odoriferous vapour, and a blonde fairy stealthily touched our shoulder, making a mock salutation, that startled us very much:—it was our playful sister, whom we complimented upon appearance and expedition; well knowing ladies to be unable to dress in a given time for a ball, whatever they may do for an opera!

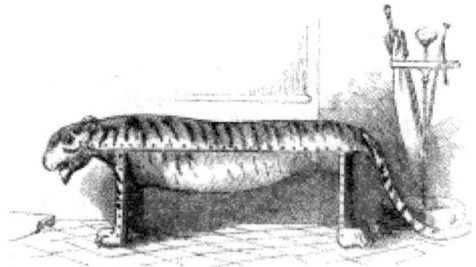

However, we had no cause for umbrage on this occasion; for the carriage rumbled over the hard, dry, ground, just as St. Stiff's was striking nine—the stars above, twinkling, as they only can, upon a clear, frosty night. Having knocked mildly, for fear of frightening Mrs. Brown thus early, and been kept waiting some time, we were admitted; after being taken for Mr. Strap, the help, by John, whom we surprised in his fustian jacket and the middle of a fugitive tea. The ladies soon disappeared into an upper region, not soon to return, leaving us to find amusement as we best could:—to examine the tiger-skin, ingeniously sewn upon a form to resemble a living animal (which, by the bye, it did not); to peep into the parlour, and discover the supper, looking mysteriously vast, by the light of one burner, very much turned down; to pace the hall; warm our kids at the Arnott; and, standing upon the mat, listen to the unsophisticated talk without—speculating as to what a foreign traveller could divine the conversation to mean, or the diurnal occupation of the lanthorn-men to be:—

1st voice. "Droves, did yer say, in Mad-ox Street?"

2nd do. "Yes, herds; I got eight bulls and a hog out of Bullstrode Street."

1st do. "See to that bull's-eye, calf; and, as there ain't no kids a-coming, I'll toss yer for a tanner."

Here "the noblest study of mankind" was broken off—Alphonso appearing. We left our men, to pace the hall—abandoning character for a slow march,—whilst the page constructed a scaffold of clothes-horses and table-covers, forming a repository for hats, over the back kitchen-stairs; the lobby beyond which, we discovered had been metamorphosed into a still-room, and was now presided over by two pretty, plump damsels, in the finest cobweb caps—mere blond buttons, of no earthly use, but, withal, very becoming:—one of these maids being in converse with a young "gent.," who, it appears, has been forgotten in the excitement, and discovered here—his face very sticky with candy and cream. Master Thomas Brown, fearing that such search might be instituted for him, has taken a great affection to the leg of the still-room table; from which he is coaxed by more attractive substances, seized, and borne up to bed—his yells becoming "small by degrees and beautifully less," until lost altogether.

Now comes Mr. Strap, to help and wait at table—in his huge white cravat, yellow vest, and new pair of second-hand plush smalls, disappearing below to develop his calves, which are enveloped in gaiters,—gingerly beckoning the man with the bad hat, who had been tuning the piano, and Mr. Palaver, the Mizzlington Artist in hair, to follow, that they may escape by the back door.

We had been promenading the hall for some time, having become pretty well acquainted with the pattern of the encaustic tiles with which it was paved; and were going towards the entrance for the last time, pluming ourself that we might appear to the greatest advantage—for we felt assured the ladies were descending, having heard a rustling and tittering;—when, just turning by the door, we were electrified by three distinct bangs, that subsided into a sharp rat, with an infinity of tail, causing the lid of the letter-box to look as if it had the palsy, and ourself to retreat like a shot— feeling alternately hot and cold; whilst Strap, who, upon hearing Mrs. Brown's footsteps, began to be very busy, performing a feat of strength with seven waiters, a copper scuttle and an ice-pail, is put in such trepidation that he loses his grip—all coming to the flags; causing the greatest amount of clamour at the smallest amount of sacrifice—Mrs. Brown saying she is happy it is not glass, and hoping Strap hasn't been drinking. The effect having annihilated the cause, the door is not opened; so the dose gets repeated, with similar gusto, by Fred. Lark—for it was he that gave the "stunner," and witnessed the commotion through the attenuated windows at either side the door,—a piece of pleasantry for which he got stigmatised by Mrs. B. as a naughty, noisome, noisy man; and for which he himself proposed the *still-room*, as an antidote. Now, Mr. Lark is one of those funny little men, rather liked, because not over given to sarcasm, and quite capable of laughing at his own jokes; or rather the jokes he has picked up and disseminates—such whimsies in their place being very well, but out of it intolerable nuisances. Mr. Lark commenced his vagaries in the still-room, when we were taking coffee, placing the toast on the table, and the buttered bread to the fire; proffering the sugar to Miss Angelina; inquiring of that lady if she *liked* her tea—because, if not, she might *lump* it; and upon our observing some cracknels, as hard, the Lark said—it was *harder* where there were none; and that evening he completely confounded Mr. Brown, by informing the worthy gentleman—he had not seen him this year!—nothing very remarkable, considering it only three days' old; but enough, withal, to make Mr. Brown think of three hundred and sixty-five—doubting the statement.

Now arrive the musicians, with a gentle knock:—up goes the harp (like a huge blade-bone in baize), followed by the cornet, violin, and pianist. We ascend:—Mrs. Brown popping and firing her parting injunctions in every direction—at Alphonso, in the (library) coffee-room; at Mr. Strap, by the door; at John, by the foot of the stairs;—and, I was going to say, at the listless supernumerary footman, lolling over the banisters; who appeared in, or rather out of, character, by especial desire, for this night only, being lent with the rout-seats at a sure salary. As Mrs. Brown passed this latter gentleman in silence, we could not help smiling—hoping she might have to think as well of his powers as he did himself, and that all titles entrusted to his care might be safely delivered; for we knew Mrs. Bramston would not be called *Brimstone*, without turning fiery; or Mr. Reynard Sly put up with anything but *Slée*, though he may write it Sly, himself.

Having gained the drawing-room, and got fairly through the muslin-barrier in the doorway, which made the staircase look as if in a fog, we found the appearance within very gratifying—everything well out of the way, and no stinting of wax-lights:—altogether exhibiting a clearer stage than is often to be met with—some antique people inviting you to polk in an old curiosity shop;—as, the other evening, at the Dowager Lady Oldbuck's, young Whisk, of the Heavies, brought down a *buhl* table, covered with porcelain gimcracks; a thing that Lark observed—ought to cure itself, if people wished to save their *Sèvres*. Evening parties are not the slow things they used to be:—here the back balcony is all evergreens and tissue-paper blossoms, lit up with a Chinese lanthorn—looking like a fairy bower, tenanted by four gaping gold-fish and a dissipated canary; the little boudoir, beyond, so snug in sage and silver, seeming but small accommodation for card-players. We thought of Lady Oldbuck's—the valuable space occupied by *chaperones* and corpulent cronies,—blessing the new mode;—dances now being given to dancers, not to dowagers and matrimonial slave-dealers, as heretofore. Mrs. Brown calculates her company; and thinking there is enough for a quadrille in either room, she commences to form them—pouncing, from time to time, upon timid young men by the door, who are led forward, like lambs from a flock, to sacrifice,—until the sets are completed—all but one couple—Mrs. Brown stating herself "distressed for ladies;"—a combination of suffering by no means acute, for she stood up herself, having engaged the amiable young Slowcoach to fill the gap.

THE QUADRILLE.

No sooner did the orchestra commence—barely having finished the first eight bars of "the Martyrs",—than the guests came rushing up from the coffee-room, like sheep through a hedge, one bolder than the rest leading the way, causing Mrs. Brown to desert her partner in _L'été_—a figure the gentleman feels bound to execute twice, though he would much rather have been excused either performance; and upon Mrs. Brown's presenting a substitute he became so beside himself as to forget the figure—a mishap rendered none the clearer by a wag's performing *la pastorale*, when he ought to have done *trenise*, and moreover, not have done it in such a facetious manner, as to render it a matter of doubt if he himself could have recognized it; the audacity being accompanied by a certain amount of shyness, that had to be hidden, altogether sadly deranging our amiable youth's comprehension, he being led by his partner, instead of leading *her*—to be left, alone, in a mental pillory, a specimen of blushing mortification more diverting to behold than to experience;—but, upon being kindly treated by his gentle partner, he recovers, in the *galop finale*, feeling truly grateful to the guardian spirit that has conducted him through the purgatory. Ladies, be gentle with youthful bashfulness—it often arises from pure feelings, modest diffidence, or unselfishness;—such, unlike many proficient dancers, carry their brains in their hats, and not in their boots:— weigh your "*fantastic-toes*" against them, and see which are the most empty.

Somehow, the first quadrille is always unfortunate!—In the back room they succeeded no better than in the front:—here, Miss Charmer was top of the dance, as she always is, if it can be obtained; especially in the *Lancers or Caledonians* (which, we dare say, are pleasant quadrilles to those who know them, and the Charmer does). Well, she is top, with young Hoy (heir to Sir Hobbedy), for a partner, a brave youth at quoits, cricket, boxing, or boating—his hands, horny as a tortoise and large as Polyphemus', over which he split three right-hand gloves:— a glance will suffice to show how much he is *out* of his, and she *in* her, element—Miss Charmer looking, Lark said, as if she would prefer performing the "first *set*" (or *sit*) upon a vacant seat, beside Arthur Beau, who has just arrived, and by whom, we know, she disliked to be quizzed;—so, upon the completion of the first eight bars, the Charmer flounced, bringing the flounces of her dress into contact with the bars of the grate, causing the smoke to come out, and Arthur to come round, that he might lean upon the shelf, engage himself for the next dance, and stand behind the fair partner, a fire-guard of honour, unable to keep from smiling at Mr. Hoy, who dances upon his heels, as though enamoured of his large feet, and afraid of knocking his head against the chandelier. Their *vis-à-vis* is a lively lady, apparently taking stock of a *bouquet*, but, in reality, joking an absent gentleman, opposite:—it is Miss Gay, whom Lark (her partner) is making laugh, by observing—the gentleman is not so *absent* as he ought to be; causing that lady to forget herself—making many mistakes and false starts; which, being those of a person who knew better, were very diverting. Miss Gay is voluble as volatile, no subject coming amiss—she is now speculating as to how far the gentlemen will permit the buttons to travel down their backs, or their skirts to be curtailed; and Mr. Lark, unable to find a reason, must get up a contrary supposition—imagining some middle-aged ladies to resemble a cork-screw, as they have at different periods shifted the waist from the armpits downward;—*waists* making us think of the short lady (in this set) with a very long one—Miss Price, only child of Alderman Price, chandler and dry-salter, of Candlewick ward—daughter and *hair*, as Mr. Lark jocosely observed, in allusion to the luxuriant red tresses of that lady:—saying her papa was the great crony of Sir Rich. Big, the free vintner, late of Portsoken ward, who was found, or rather not found—having evaporated of spontaneous combustion, before he could get to the civic chair,—leaving all his money to Price; who has retired, with his fat and the gout, to Bayswater. Miss Price is a lovely dancer, appearing hollow (a thing Miss Gay did not doubt), like an India rubber ball in flounces; she is said to have a beautiful hand, so small as to require only No. 6. gloves—as if a pigmy hand could not be a deformity. She is invited, in a hope that young Brown may make her a partner, for the dance of life; and is said to be worth £150,000—not by the pound weight, as the envious Miss Gay hinted.—No! No! naughty Miss Gay, be satisfied with Nature's gifts, and do not covet lucre.

Here comes young Brown, who has not danced before, to make arrangements with Miss Gay, who has—and proved herself the *belle* of the room;—but, as gentlemen are now in the minority, she does not hint at being "engaged for the next," or propose "the one after."

There is a temporary lull, after the dance:—and in comes Captain de Camp, looking like a macaw in a dress-coat, leading Lady Lucretia de Camp, who resembles an apoplectic canary—so glittering is the amber satin,—followed by the sons, who meander amongst the beaux and bare shoulders, in search of the Miss Browns—dancing with no one else all the evening,—causing the gentlemen to think very little of the De Camps, and the ladies less of the Miss Browns. Now, then, for a polka!—the rattling "Post knock Polka!"—Off! away they go, after a great deal of reluctance and playful diffidence as to who should lead off—Miss Charmer with Arthur Beau, twirling round and round, in and out (like an eel among skittles); followed by Mr. Latimer and Miss Jemima, who evidently intended to do great things, but only cause confusions and contusions, until they get knocked into the open space, in the centre of the human vortex—the Charmer spinning, as a top that could not stop, while the music continued, like the automata in front of a street organ. There, there they go!—that is Lord Towney—he who came with Mr. Serjeant Wideawake, the Honourable Member for Bloomsbury—the fellow who got acquainted with Brown, as brother-director of the "Dodo Assurance," that didn't do, and was done up. His Lordship is son of the Marquis of Mary-le-bone—he that is flying with the pink flounces,—the buoyant, hollow, Miss Price, whose pretty button of a nose we do believe

was impressed with the basket-work on her partner's fourth shirt-stud. Round and round they twist—backwards, forwards, and sideways,—between parties parted, and openings that close again,—faster and faster,—smiling, frowning, and apologizing,—growing swifter and swifter,—until the floor snapped, and rebounded with an awful crash.

****

The visitors are in the room below—a scene of ruin and rueful faces;—the supper that was displayed there, in all its state, is done for. Alas!—the chandelier has been polked off the hook—a mishap in which few sympathise, for the floor is said to be safe; Mr. Lark being the first to propose their going above, as he jokingly observed—to crack the *party*-wall. Now, for that vastly-relished valse, the "Teetotum"—liked none the less for the late excitement!—*deux temps* against *trois temps*—the latter getting worsted; and the Brown girls, who danced every dance, with certain gentlemen, only, more and more unpopular.

As the evening progresses, the wall-flowers become bolder;—some finding partners for quadrilles; others edging up to the vacant recesses, rendering it now possible to get out at the door, and obtain air on the landing—where several young fellows are congregated:—there young Lark was laughing, we knew, at the Rev. Jewel St. Jones, the clerk in orders at St. Stiffs, doing the *cavalier seul*—for we heard him say something about early missal, or primitive Christian style,—joking the reverend gentleman's partner, Miss what's-her-name, the "lamp-post," from No. 4, Bury Court, St. Mary Axe—that washed-out, faint, fair creature,—she, that looks as if you could see the back buttons of her dress through from the front—that lady—well, do you see her?—It is said her mother keeps her in a dark closet, that she may look like a consumptive geranium:—however, Mr. Lark said *he* did not believe it; and, as no one said they did, the matter ended. The stairs soon become a popular observatory—several Wall-flowers joining the knot; one of whom mildly remarks something about three silver-grey silks, in the fore-ground, and their being "much worn;" which Mr. Lark fully agreed in, as, he said, they appeared to have been *turned* several times—a joke, at which the Wall-flower faintly smiles, for the three silver-greys are his sisters:—however, nothing daunted, he is at it again, remarking upon marriage, and people that look married; illustrating his theory by pointing out the juvenility of an aunt, who he says is a virgin:—Lark retorting—"*virging* on fifty!"— a notification that begets much laughter, making the Wall-flower feel at a discount, and more than ever desire to say something smart; so, he pitches upon a gentleman with parenthetical (bowed) legs, observing that Brown has invited his tailor; moreover, wagering two to one, that if the gentleman, so libelled, were asked to look at the splashes on the calf of his leg, he would take it up in front, and examine it in his hand, like a nabob or tailor, used to sit upon the floor; were he a Christian, he would look at it over his shoulder:—here the Wall-flower turned for applause, looking over his own shoulder to illustrate the anecdote—there to discover, Captain de Camp, the gentleman who introduced "Parenthesis," a staff doctor, from Woolwich (at least so the Captain said). But here we will leave them to proceed below, and see how matters progress in the supper-room:—

The chandelier, the treacherous culprit, that would not swing or hang in chains, is being borne away, clanking along the lower hall; the broken glass has been picked out of the pastry, and the oily odour overcome with *esprit de bouquet*—presenting, withal, a very effective *coup-d'œil*:—though, we could fancy the tipsy-cake, in the form of a leaning-tower, if anything, a little more groggy; and that the composite Corinthian temple looked as if it had suffered from an earthquake—but there it was, for all the intense remorse of the cook, who thought the exhibition of so mutilated a work of art would injure his reputation for ever—but it did not!—Neither did any one notice the loss of the frail effeminate brigand, that formerly tenanted the rotunda of barley-sugar; nor was it known that a treadmill had given place to a locomotive and tender—in sweets.

The first portion of this banquet disappears merrily; there being no lack of the usual conserves, pasties, and geometrical bread-envelopes—supposed to contain something, but consumed without the slightest knowledge of their contents.

After the ladies have supped and withdrawn, the gentlemen lay to, with immense energy, as if to make up for the time they have been kept in suspense, creating great havoc amongst ruined fowls, or anything they can lay hands upon—in the excitement, particularity having given place to mirth. One gentleman has planted a spoon in his button-hole, after the fashion of a flower; and, of course, for his pains, got called a "Spooney," by an unknown voice behind Mr. Potts, the tame apothecary, who is pouring, or rather measuring out, some champagne, *himself*, catching the final drop on the edge of the glass, as if it were castor-oil:—the "Spooney," thinking it Potts' voice, must make a joke in return; so begins with the rather hackney'd, but, as he thought, appropriate one, of *champagne* being better than *real* pain or *quinine wine*; and, upon Mr. P.'s essaying to answer, our "Spoon" diverted to some tongue he was consuming, saying he liked it better than *Potted tongue*—an observation that made the apothecary's face flush, and the "Spoon" liken it to an article before them, a *claret-mug*. At this last allusion the "Pott" got red-hot, and there is no knowing what would have been the consequences, had not the "Spoon" terrified the "Pott" by proclaiming "silence!"—in a stentorian voice;—and a gentleman risen, Dr. Portbin, the author of that elaborate essay on "Dribbling Babies," in one thick volume, royal octavo—a work that nobody read, but everybody thought a great deal of, for it gained its author a vast infantine practice:—so, when the M.D. rose, the "Pott" trembled—feeling greatly relieved to find the doctor only did so to propose the "ladies"—"health and long life to Mrs. Brown and the ladies!"—a toast that was drunk with great enthusiasm, Mr. Lark vociferously applauding; at the same time stating, in an under tone—"the doctor meant a long life of ills and bills." Dr. Portbin's sentiment is echoed by Mr. Brown, who returns thanks in a stereotype-speech, almost as original as a royal one; to which, in some points, it bore slight resemblance, the ideas being very much generalized—there was an "alliance with foreign powers," "acquisition of territory," and "friendly relations:"—altogether a prosperous allegory, which causes Captain de Camp to be "called upon;" and, in that style of speech usually denominated "neat," give very visible vent to his inexpressible feelings—sketching several scenes, commencing at Victoria Villa and ending at St. Stephen's,—with a verse, intended to look as if composed for the nonce; but, in reality, a work of much study:—it was delivered with great emphasis—a composition for which we had to blush, though, as faithful chroniclers, feel bound to insert—it ran as follows:—

"Victoria and Albert's big

With city's wealth and soldier's glory:

75

To Army, Queen, and Country swig:

Improve, my friends, and prove the Tory!"

We do not think the Captain quite liked the word "swig," but he could find no better in "Walker's Rhyming Dictionary;" or the last expression—but *Conservative* could not be lugged in any how:—however, we must say, this ostensible improvisatorial effort produced a grand effect, and a greater noise; which had scarcely subsided, when Mr. Serjeant Wideawake, the Honourable Member for Bloomsbury, and author of "Lays of a Liberal," rose to retort, saying,—

"We beg to doubt your precious rig,

And I'll tell you another story:

To *improve* is to be a *whig*;

But not to *improve-is-a-tory*!"

The effect of this latter burst of poetic fire was truly electric; it completely extinguished the Captain's impromptu glimmer, lighting up that gallant bosom with a passion of another kind— he feels miserably "put out;"—and, like a dying rush-light in its last moments, seemed determined to end with a spark of unusual brightness. The Captain stood erect, awaiting his opportunity; but, alas!—it was one that never came; for the ventriloquist, that caused the rupture between Mr. Potts and the "Spooney," made the "Lion" wince, by observing, "he hoped there would be no cruelty to animals"—a remark that made our "Lion" roar contemptuously

and call the company "bears and monkeys"—he growling, with blood-thirsty pugnacity, about "satisfaction" and "Chalk Farm,"—the declamatory mania causing the irascible monster to mount a projection in the recess, covered with a curtain, bringing down an avalanche of fenders, fire-irons, and other stowage, with a fearful crash—crowning the "king of beasts" with a helmet-scuttle,—thus permitting the meaner animals to escape; leaving, as Mr. Lark (who came out last) said, between frightful gusts of laughter oozing from his handkerchief, Jackall Brown, the lion's provider, pacifying the enraged brute with claret or soda water; and John in such an extreme fit of awe, that he has taken the state jug, with the hole in the bottom stopped with sealing-wax—only intended to hold cold water, into use, for hot; and, being unable to stop the orifice with his finger, drops the article—to the scalding of the already enfuriated "Lion."

******

Feet were pattering above as we left this scene of strife—no time seeming to have been lost during the consumption of the supper; for the hands of the clock, in the hall, pointed to an earlier hour than they did when we descended:—the truth being, Lark, though rather fast himself, thought Time too much so, and put him back a little. The Wall-flower is comparing the clock with his repeater. Lark is reprimanding him, saying—it is not *etiquette* to do so; and that really some one ought to tell the vulgar thing, in green satin, who wore her button of a watch-face outward (fearing lest it should be taken for a locket), to turn the bauble round, for it is time she was in bed.

Having been absent for a short period, we were informed by the Lark that we had *not* lost a treat—for Jemima had been singing, "Memory, be thou ever true!"—whilst Lark (perpetrating a dreary pun) said, he every moment wished the music-stool would prove a *fall setto*, and precipitate the lady to the ground; for it was a sad pity to hear poor Spohf's songs so murdered.

They are now at a waltz—"the Olga,"—which is carried on with spirit, lasting a very long while—young Lark saying he does not waltz, for it makes his head swim; and that he has an objection to stand holding by the shelf, experiencing a sensation delightful as standing upon one's head in a swing, before a lady that ought to have your best attention;—however, for all Lark's protestations, we saw some one-sided smiles, as much as to say, *his* vulnerable part, like that of Achilles, lay in the heels—an insinuation Lark could well afford to allow, for he does not live to *dance*, alone, like some sage, perfect, performers.

After the "Caledonians" and another polk (which, for diversion, young Brown has danced to the tune of the "College-hornpipe"—a pleasing eccentricity), followed a quadrille, *à la Française*, danced without sides, in two very long lines—a style reported to have been imported from a Casino, and not held to be proper by sober people. So, Potts got a disgust for the polka, and thought *it* improper—a dance he never patronised or wished to—it being too *fast* for the dull apothecary!—he hated it, because once an inveterate polkist nearly knocked his *patella*, or knee-pan, off, with some hard substance in the flying tails of the dancer's dress-coat—a huge street-door key, that ought to have been left in the *paletôt*.

Our evening is drawing to a close:—the mouths in the boudoir are assuming the shape of elongated O's—an epidemic that has extended to the Wall-flowers; the "harp" has accompanied his instrument with fitful snores; the "violin" scarcely knows the back from the front of his fiddle, or the "cornet" which end to blow into;—yet, upon being asked for "Roger de Coverley," they make a desperate effort to awake, for they know it to be the last dance—which is supported by the whole strength of the company,—Captain de Camp leading off with Mrs. Brown, and Mr. Brown with Lady Lucretia. Thus ends the Christmas Ball!

The still-room is being besieged for coffee; and there is a great difficulty in obtaining hats and coats—unfortunately few of the tickets corresponding,—for Alphonso's ward was precipitated down the kitchen stairs, it having been too heavily laden. Lady and Miss Highbury are seen to their carriage by Mr. Lark, who departs in Lord Towney's cab, with a "*Gibus*" hat, mechanically deranged—all wrinkles, like a jockey's boot. Upon being asked, by a lanthorn-bearer, "if his Honor has such a thing as a pint o' beer in his pocket?" Mr. Lark, with playful irony, informs the supernumerary that malt liquor is not a solid, neither is it to be obtained at evening parties.

To and fro, flit the Jack-o'-lanthorns, respectfully touching the binding of their battered hats, covering the tiers of muddy wheels with their coat-tails, that the *tulle* and *tartelaine* may not be spoiled—hoping your Honour will "remember" them!—as they cast uncertain shadows upon the icy pavement—ice that has been rendered none the less slippery by their cutting out a slide upon it, with the assistance of the police, during the evening:—such a banging of doors, clashing of steps, and stopping up the way, under the little awning, over the carriage-sweep—a pretty pass, so narrow that, we are sorry to say, the hackney-drivers instituted a private road amongst the hardy shrubs, choking up the gates, to the great distress of pedestrians, who are looked upon by the "lanthorns" as "shabby gents,"—paying nothing for the privilege of walking;—they (the "lanthorns") viewing the immunity, in the light of parsimony. However, we think walking home, after a party, under the influence of champagne, a dangerous experiment:—the clear free streets seeming to court a "lark," and the very bells to invite pulling—"Visitors'," and "Night," "Knock and Ring," (and run) also.

We have since heard the fate of a rash expedition undertaken at this season, the band of adventurers consisting mostly of those gentlemen who had passed the last half-hour dying for a cigar; and yet, by some unknown attractive power, felt bound to stay the entertainment out—probably it was that such kindred souls might depart *en masse*; however, be it what it might, their first care was to obtain a light—at some sacrifice, for the lamp-post had been newly painted; and, secondly, happening to pass Mr. Spohf's, they must serenade that gentleman with pathetic negro-melodies—about the loss of one "Mary Blane," and an injunction to "Susannah" not to sob,—until driven by the police into another beat, there to lose one of their band, who fell a victim to an inquiring spirit;—for, seeing an inscription on a door, to intimate that its owner, a surgeon, gave "advice, gratis, between the hours of four and five, every Saturday," he rang to demand the same (having the head-ache), as it was just that time by St. Stiff's; but, unfortunately falling into the clutches of No. 8, of the A division, he had to receive the advice, from a magistrate, between eleven and twelve, at a fee of five shillings.

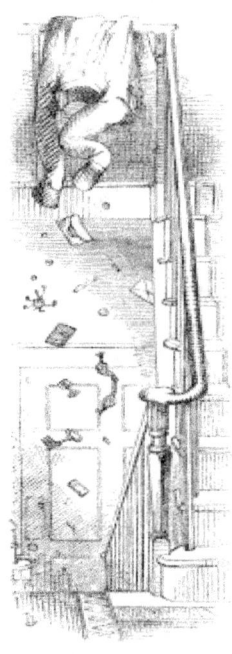

We left Mr. Lark in Lord Towney's cab—again to take up with him, being put down at the end of Bloomsbury Buildings, fearing the rattle of wheels in that quiet *cul-de-sac* would disturb the old Larks. Having found the door, and spent five minutes by the hinges—searching for the key-hole, he gets within; and spends five more—trying to ignite an extinguisher;—cautiously stealing to bed, throwing his *paletôt* over the top banister, and the contents of its pockets down the well-staircase, to the awakening of the whole house.

At Victoria Villa the last guest has gone:—the De Camps have gone—departed with cordiality and love for all that is Brown, at the same time sadly mortified with the impression made on that worthy gentleman's friends. Mrs. Brown, worn out and exhausted, has given a parting glance round, with her night-lamp, and panted up to-bed; the Misses Brown have retired to their chambers; John feels very much inclined to proclaim his opinion of the Captain, but is fearful of the consequences; and Mr. Strap, who has fallen a victim to his weak point—strong drink, is rendered thereby quite incapable of making either a base to his person, or a fluent speech, as it seems he wished; for, upon meeting Mr. Brown by the stairs, he made a rush at the esteemed proprietor of that name, prophetically bidding him to "B-B-Beware of Captings in w-w-w-wolf's clo-o-othing, fur all isn't gug-gug-gold as gl-l-l-litters, as the Rev-rind Miss-s-s-ster B-B-Bucket observes, in the Proverbs of Sol'mon's songs." Mr. Strap, after having delivered these sentiments, in what might have been called a *sotto* voice, to an imaginary Mr. Brown (for the reality had withdrawn to bed), performs an unsuccessful backward movement upon his heels—as if to survey his victim,—coming to the ground; where he lay until borne off by John, who thinks him a valiant fool.

The persevering Brown, though much fatigued, does not postpone the Diary:—"January 4th, Friday—*Execrable* Friday!—We this day gave our Annual Ball—*we*, indeed!—why I knew nothing about it until all the cards had been despatched. Mrs. Brown asks—just as Tom does, if he may have the sugar, when it is half consumed:—It was Mrs. Brown's *ball* in every sense. I did hope to have experienced more enjoyment for the money. I have many a time been happier at half the price;—ay, happier when I was clerk at Chizzle and Filch's, in Aldermanbury; but, somehow, I suppose a man must make sacrifices for his friends, as penurious old

Chizzle did, when he paid the debt of nature, and left to me *that* he could not take away! Not that I ever made any sacrifices for Spohf—no, *he* never asked it;—cheap trusty friendship is *something!*—I must own to feeling, all the evening, as if my collar had too much starch therein; and more out of place in my own house than the 'white neckerchiefs' that waited at supper. I am like a fish out of water, and that fish, a flat-fish—caught with a bit of red ray; however, there must be a great deal in use—another element may be delightful, when used to it. There is no doubt my old friend Wideawake's attack upon the Captain was mere envy; and as to his insinuating that I should never eat a peck of salt with *that* man—to say I shall never know *that* man, is preposterous!—as to eating the literal peck, no man, probably, will do that; for the Captain has an aversion to saline food, saying it makes the bones soft. I wonder if it has the same effect upon brains!—We shall see, Wideawake—we *shall* see:—let this page bear testimony! I hope the briny ocean may not swallow up the Captain's luggage."

Victoria and Albert slumber late on the morning of the 5th:—Alphonso is the first up—or rather down, having rolled off his uncomfortable bed, constructed upon four chairs, in the drawing-room. Mrs. Brown, too, must have risen on the wrong side of her teaser, so testy is she this morning—thanking her stars that Twelfth-day has arrived, to put an end to the Christmas miseries!—Soon, now, will that little pest, Tom, be packed back to "Tortwhack House;" and the juvenile party, of to-day, it is hoped may appease some rampant mammas uninvited to the grand *réunion*—rendering any petty excuses that may be given the more feasible.

The day rolls rapidly away, though not with half the speed Master Brown could desire—the hands of the hall-clock appearing to creep so, that every time Tom passed it (and that was not seldom), he stopped to see if it was going, the day seeming most unusually long, and night as if it never would come; but it did!—firstly, bringing the little "Merrys," from Hope Cottage, the Tudor lodge, next-door-but-one—Master Walter Merry being the first to answer Tommy's nubbly note of invitation, in intoxicated text capitals, that appeared to be making a desperate effort to run off the paper, at the right-hand corner, leaving no room to "remain," and scarcely any to "please turn over;" so folded was it, to give the desired angular form, that the paper looked as if it had been used to make five hundred geometrical cocks and boats.

Tom met the Merrys with such fervent joy, that he never thought they had healths, or anything else to ask after; his only object, seeming to be the finding of his friend, who is rolled, like a mummy, in numberless boas and shawls:—during the process of unswathing, which was no easy job to one in a hurry, so artfully were the pins introduced, Master Tommy treats his friend Walter to a railroad retrospective review of the good things in store—recounting all the "lummy" things left yesterday;—telling about the "nobby" Christmas tree Captain de Camp gave them—though his ma' did say it was "a pretty give!"—it was stolen out of *his* father's garden.—My father's a jolly sight richer than your's—he has more trees in his garden—ain't we got a "swag" of nuts, and a "plummy" twelfth-cake—my father won it at an art-union, in the city! I am to draw King—if I don't, just see how I'll cry!—Mercy Merry shall be Queen. You shall have Punch off the cake; and ma'says I shall have "Rule Britannia," as soon as the waves and ice have melted away.

Now a knock brings more visitors, the Masters Young, in all the ungainliness of hobbledyhoyhood—that transmigratory period when coat-tails are first developed:—they have come with their sister Flora, a lovely bud, expected "out" next season. Here are the Bells, the Petits, and the little Larks, with their big brother, the "jolly Lark," who made his *début* over the top of the drawing-room-door, standing upon the shoulders of your humble servant; who felt the "jolly Lark" anything but light, and no joke—though the juveniles must have thought it so, for we could hear their merry peals of laughter ringing joyously, dispelling the silence that had hitherto prevailed, overturning the sage injunctions of *proper* mammas, who teach their children to behave "pretty"—thinking *good* and *quiet* synonymous. Somehow, the little fellows, unfortunately, take the Lark for Mr. Spohf, who has hitherto done the funny in a refined style, scarcely to be imagined—an elegant, amiable, fun,—a mixture of the buffoon and gentleman, the sublime and the ridiculous, quite marvellous to behold,—making our little friend (who you are aware was moulded in one of Nature's odd freaks) appear, to tender imaginations, almost supernatural. The mistake and misplaced approbation is very galling to Mrs. Brown; so much so that she becomes angry with the tea-urn, and, in turn, burns her fingers—venting her ire in the shape of a box on the ears of Master Bold, who ventured to hint Mr. Spohf's absence a "jolly shame;" and, now vows to tell his mamma—a thing it is very evident Mrs. Brown does not wish, for she has shown a great deal of favour and contrition towards the young gentleman since.

The tea-tray having been removed, the burners of the chandelier heightened, and the Snuffle family had their row of little noses polished by the eldest sister, preparations begin:—Miss Jemima playing the pretty little "Hop o'my Thumb Polka," and Tom, who has been sitting very quietly beside Mercy Merry (vowing to marry her at fourteen, for "his father is so rich that he would give him five pounds a year to live upon"), leads off, much to the mortification of those boys who will not be "young gentlemen"—the many who won't, can't, and shan't dance! but, being bent upon mischief, dispose explosive spiders and chair-crackers about the carpet;—one little mischievous fellow wishing he had brought some pepper to strew on the floor, and make 'em sneeze; however, they get up a little excitement another way with the sofa-pillows, a sham fight, in which a parian Amazon falls beside Marian Bell, who "didn't go to do it;" so dancing is relinquished for games to suit all parties:—Hunt the Slipper, a sport carried on with great spirit, until it is found there are slippers enough for three—a thing everybody holds to be cheatery:—so that game is abandoned for Blind-man's-buff, the mere mention of which, carries us back to childhood; and, as authors often lug in their thoughts (bits of nature) very unceremoniously, and at odd times, we may, possibly, be pardoned or praised for so doing. Well, we never hear mention of this game but we think of a bump we once received during the sport, our blind ardour causing us to flounder in a fender, and bruise our head, the remains of which will be taken to the "long home." Well do we remember the spotted turban worn on that occasion—for we recollect, at the time, thinking "Belcher" a new term, just coined;—having our crown rubbed with brandy and taking a little internally, which appeared attracted by that externally, for it got in our head and made us very merry, causing the hiccups to such an extent, that we were called *Sir Toby Belch* of "Twelfth Night; or, What you Will" notoriety (having drawn that character). Thus, brandy, Belchers, and Blind-man's-buff, hold an indissoluble partnership in our memory—a remnant of those days when we imagined a Jew incapable of dealing in other merchandise than old clothes; or of shaving like a Christian, or, if he did, would do other than expose a pendant chin, resembling the *vertebræ* of a horse's tail. Oh! those days have flown—days when we imagined peas split by hand, and thought humanity fools for not making soup with whole ones—but we are sadly digressing!—"It's not fair!" cry twenty voices—"the blind man can see;" and so he could, for he always caught Miss Brown, who, afraid of the piano or pier-glass, would stand in the way:—so that sport is relinquished for cake and Characters; the former seeming to afford great gratification, and the latter little, save to the King and Queen—all other characters

being, like the riddles,   "given up,"— no one caring to know when a sailor is not a sailor?—when he's a-board: or to be bored with a door's being a-jar, and a man a-shaving.

The rich cake is soon a ruin; so much is every part of it relished, that one young gentleman has consumed the head and shoulders of Madame Alboni, under a delusion of her being sugar, and not "plaster of parish," as Mrs. Brown afterwards said it was. The little fellows soon get very mirthful on the ginger-wine; keeping up a continual buzz, like a colony of bees, sadly itching to be at something—a wish that is not to be realized at once, for little Miss Newsoince is going to do that eternal tattoo, the "*Rataplan:*"—yes, there she is, in Tom's felt-hat and polonaise, as "*La Vivandière,*" thumping upon an empty band-box with two knitting-pins, singing, as some of the mammas say, very prettily; but as the boys, who have heard it many times before, designate it "a jolly bother!"—"a great big shame!"—"a precious dummy set out!"—and so on,—there being no *fun* in it.

This hum-drum over, a great cry is raised for *Forfeits!*—and a desire that *a lady* should *go out in a very great hurry*, as it would appear, almost in a state of destitution; for every young lady and gentleman proffers to stand for some article of dress. Having settled what they will give, all sit round upon chairs, ready to hear the *lady's* demands:—spin goes the trencher, and she wants her *Stockings!*—forward fly the hose, personated by a little fellow, with mottled legs, who had never stood in other than socks, but for all that can catch the revolving waiter, look slyly at *Bonnet*, make him think it his turn, and impudently call out *"Cap!!"*—so *Bonnet* and *Cap* knock head to head, tumble on the trencher, and get fined. *Bonnet* shouts *"Boots!"*—*Boots* begets *"Bustle!"*—and *Bustle* begets a grand stir, by calling *"Double Toilet!"*—causing the whole wardrobe to leap from every chair, in every direction, a general confusion,—in which the *Boa* slips off his seat, and forfeits a twenty-bladed knife. The *Boa*, spinning the tray again, calls *"Muff!"*—who, not being on the alert, arrives when the waiter has wabbled its last, so the *Muff* has to pay a forfeit; but having nothing eligible upon his person, is found a substitute, in a very ugly China pug-dog, afterwards called *"a very pretty thing"* by Miss Angelina to Miss Jemima, who awarded the penalties, like a blind Justice saying her prayers, passing sentence, in the lap of the judge, who demands—*"Here's a pretty thing, a very pretty thing; and what is the owner of this very pretty thing to be done to?"*

HERE'S A LADY GOING OUT, IN A
VERY GREAT HURRY, AND SHE WANTS—

Angelina sentencing the owner of the pretty pug to take a very pretty young lady into the corner, and spell "op-por-tu-ni-ty"— a spell the *Muff* does not seem to know lies in taking the *opportunity* to kiss the fair one, though he has all the evening been admiring her vastly, and would have given anything for such a chance; but next, having to "*lie the length of a looby, the breadth of a booby,*" &c., he is eminently successful—yet, who shall say the ungainly cub may not one day be an ornament to society! Poor *Muff!* he has no mother or sisters—the only specimens of girlhood known to him are the maids at home, and the school-master's daughter, that dines with the parlour-boarders at Addle House:—brave boy, thou art clever, but semi-civilized! More "*pretty things*" are being redeemed—fans, gloves, lockets, handkerchiefs, and chatelaines,—all their owners being appropriately "done to:"—the *Boa* condemned to "bite a yard off the poker;" and the *Visite* to "salute the one he likes best"—which *Garters* fancies will be her; so, she embraces the table-pillar, and he the *Berthe*, instead—kissing her, sadly to the mortification of *Garters*, who did think the honour worth some trouble. Jemima and Angelina, having disposed of the judicial pawn-brokering establishment, stroke down their skirts, and send round the currant-wine; whilst Master Tom and a few other daring youths consume lighted candle-ends, made of turnip, with almond wicks; and the merry little man, Lark, who can no more be quiet than a robin in a rat-trap, is now hopping with a paper tail, composed of this evening's "*Sun*"—a sun that seems to be incombustible, for the boys are trying to ignite it, but cannot,—only waxing Mr. Lark's pantaloons very much in the rear, and putting the candles out—a trick that caused no end of diversion, not only to the performers, but to every one; who laughed immoderately, more particularly when Mr. Lark led down Mrs. Brown to supper, the antimacassar adhering to his trowsers—the wax, upon sitting down, causing it to stick there.

This brings us to the supper-table, and the Christmas tree, with its blossoms of light—a very peculiar species of shrub:—we have heard of box-trees, plane-trees, lady's slippers, and sun-flowers, but never remember to have seen or heard of a toy and candle-tree, figured in any work on botany; nor should we have thought our little friends had ever beheld one before, for the brilliant supper seemed but small attraction compared with the illuminated fir—all eyes appeared attracted to the quarter in which it stood; and when the youthful company were introduced to it, after the banquet, we felt glad the lower boughs were out of the reach of the younger branches, or they might, in their eagerness, have pulled it out of the disguised tub. As it was, some of the recipients took the fruit intended for others:—for instance, Stephen Sharp ate all Miss Standby's basket of sweets, and then demanded the story-book that had his name attached to it. All the fruit was not edible, for we saw an apple that tasted very much of the wood, being full of pips resembling doll's tea-things; whilst, upon suction, the pears emitted musical sounds; and a biffin, like a pincushion, had the flavour of bran—probably it was bran-new.

THE CHRISTMAS TREE.

The tree, now stript, is quite devoid of interest; for, upon Mr. Lark's starting some fun in the corner, none lingered by, not even to listen to the bird-organ, that appeared to play under the table. Yes! there was Lark, at it again—doing anything to please!— Generous Lark!—his face covered with a white handkerchief, a portion tucked in his mouth, over all wearing a pair of spectacles, with pupils (currants abstracted 84from a mince-pie) stuck thereon, causing the Lark to look very curious and odd—the children wondering what he will be at next!—for now, you must know, he has gone to prepare another excitement; being in the drawing-room, whilst the visitors are in the parlour—curious

beyond all description,   beseeching the junior Mr. Brown, who is standing with his back against the door, to prevent egress, just to permit them to depart; which, after a slight contest, he does—they rushing, pell-mell, to the drawing-room, there to find an old birch-broom blazing in the grate, and the recess covered with two sheets suspended by forks. In front of the sheets is a table; whilst in front of that table, stand the wondering little crowd, speculating as to what the burning broom can have to do with it, when a dwarf old dame appears, through a slit in the drapery—as perfect a dwarf as ever breathed,—but three feet high, and so really true that no one for a moment doubts her identity or vitality. "She is a Witch!" cry all, that has come down the chimney. The dame bows acquiescence, with numberless courtseys, telling the little company of her immense age and adventures—recounting her history:—about the large family she kept in the shoe; about the refractory pig, that would not get over the stile; and her wonderful travels, to sweep cobwebs from the sky; so, after having danced a hornpipe; deplored the loss of her carriage (*broom*); demanded the grunting pig, behind the curtain, to be quiet; and scraped an infinity of courtseys, she vanishes:—the sharpest boy in the room, Muster Bold, rushing down stairs to catch a glimpse of her, but only seeing us, in our shirt sleeves, wonders the more!—*par parenthèse*—we were one of the performers, escaping, to make room for the Galanti show. So, whilst we leave the company to be amused thereby, we will, with the kind permission of Mr. Lark, instruct you how to construct an old dame; and afterwards tell the effect it had upon our audience:—

Firstly, procure a pair of small shoes and stockings—these place upon your hands (which are to represent feet); next, tie round your neck a short coloured pinafore, reaching down to your hands (or rather the old dame's feet)—this will represent a gown; now, place your shoed hands upon a table, to see effect; gird the gown with a proportionate apron, the strings of which will bind your arms and body together at the chest; put on a false nose, a pair of spectacles, a lady's frilled night-cap, and a comical conical hat; add a little red cloak, and draw the table up to a window or recess, the curtains of which pin at the back of your shoulders; and standing thus, with your hands (the old dame's feet) upon the table, you will represent the most perfect little dwarf (without arms) you can imagine; the hands are to be supplied by an accomplice, behind the curtain, who is to suit the action of those hands to the pleasantries you may invent. Thus, having given the necessary instructions, we leave the rest to be supplied by the actor; who may, if he pleases, render the old dame a medium of much merry conceit and pleasant mirth. Well do we remember the impression made at this party; for, as before stated, we performed the arms from behind the curtain, through which we occasionally peeped, getting a good view over the shoulders of Mr. Lark (the old dame), witnessing the astonished gaping gaze of the servant, who happened to enter the apartment at the moment, and stood transfixed to the spot, until the effigy had escaped. One little boy was so impressed with the illusion, that he actually went below, with some venturesome companions, in search of her; but soon returned, rushing up stairs in a state of extreme terror, declaring to us (as he kept his eyes towards the door, fearing every moment she would appear), that he had seen the old dame, and heard her pig; the truth being, one of the party had grunted in a dark corner of the lobby, and frightened the youth, who eventually became a prey to intense mental anxiety—a trembling fear we attempted to dispel, without success, until we bore the little fellow below, he clinging tightly to us. In the lobby Mr. Lark showed the scared youth our trick, piece-meal—in the end, pacifying the young gentleman, though much do we think the old dame and her pig will never be forgotten by him:—he may grow to manhood, have children, loves and cares innumerable, traverse the seas, know war and famine, yet do we think the old dame will stand boldly out, like a giant image in the desert of the past—far more so than the Galanti show, exhibited afterwards, because really alive, and capable of reason!—

Though, we had more reason to remember the show; for, the men who performed it hung their hats and coats beside Mr. Lark's, and our own; which, upon leaving, they did not identify:—though, we think they ought; as ours were considerably newer—one of their hats being a cap, and the other of dirty white felt!

After the departure of the show, we got up some sport with the sheets upon which it had been performed, exhibiting our eyes through a hole, therein; those on the obverse trying to guess the proprietor of others on the reverse—all the owners of bright eyes much enjoying the sport. But to recount the many pranks played by youthful blood that evening, would require a volume— everybody proposing everything; and everybody else, disliking the thing proposed, suggests some other:—one wanting Hunt the Whistle; a second, to act Charades; and a third, some practical joke of the old school, such as the game we played with Mr. Lark, called Porcelain Mesmerism, deceiving the little innocents into a belief that men are simple—much more so than they will find them, upon arriving at maturity!—There we sat (two full-grown fools) staring at each other, with plates of water in our hands, the bottom of one sooty, the other clean!—There we sat, face to face, alternately rubbing the bottoms of the plates, and stroking our physiognomies, in mockery of each other—Mr. Lark getting his face blacked like a sweep,—the youngsters laughing at his silliness!—Oh, that a little smut should produce such ecstatic mirth!

There is Walter Merry, looking like an eel in convulsions—imagining he has been here about an hour:—you should have seen the expression of the little fellow, when Mrs. Brown gently tapped him on the shoulder, saying, "Master Merry, you're fetched!" Time was annihilated, and memory dumbfounded!—The entertainment that had been looked forward to for days, counted by the hours, and put so many mammas in a pother, is gone!—The hands of the hall-clock are almost perpendicular—it wants but half-an-hour of midnight!—Several

MASTER MERRY AS HE APPEARED

anxious mammas WHEN HE WAS "FETCHED"!!! have sent several times for their several little ones; and the several servants have been sent away with several evasive answers—for "the little dears are enjoying themselves so much!"—"Mrs. Brown's compliments to Mrs. Fidgets, and would she permit the little Fidgets to stay just ten minutes longer?" No!—the Fidgety footman is only to depart *with* them; so he is sent to the servants' hall, there to wait, whilst snap-dragon is being prepared in the library—that the evening may end with a grand blue-fire *tableaux*. The room resembles the Black Hole of Calcutta!—Hundreds of little itching fingers are longing to be amongst that pound of raisins, in spirits—all eager, as imps, for the fiendish sport; the darkness and suspense rendering it very exciting—causing Master Jewel (a model boy), who is "wanted directly," to make no answer from the sable mass; until, the summons being repeated, he says something that sounds very like "shan't come!"—and, Master

Jewel does not come, until he has had his portion of the fiery food that is flying about in every direction.

END OF JUVENILE PARTY,
MASTER BROWN FEELS AS IF HE HAD
HAD A GOOD MANY GOOD THINGS.

During the last hour Cook and John have held a *soirée* below, to all the neighbouring domestics, who are awaiting to escort home their little masters and mistresses—they are regaling upon ale and sandwiches, in the servants' hall; whilst that most interesting topic, "every body's business," is being discussed:—Mrs. Pest's maid assuring all, upon her sacred word and honour, that Mrs. Pest is not a angel, or the "Pest-house" a paradise, though it may look pretty over the garden-wall; and, moreover, Mrs. P.'s maid said she were of opinion the public knowed it, too; for t'other night some one painted out the fust letters, ag'in our door-post—making the direction, at the corner of the lane, "Placid Vale," read *"acid ale"* instead,—no compliment, as the maid said, to Mr. "Pest, Pewter, and Co.'s Entire;"—at the same time observing, that it sarved 'em right! And, "as I hope, afore next Heaster, to lose my blessed Virgin Mary name, I'd go—if it wer'n't for the pale-ale-tory circumstances, I'd warn Missus! It was only yesterday, jist arter Mr. Pest had gone to Brewhus, in Liquorish St., that we had a scrimmage about flounces; and jist as I was a-going to fling my resignation at her—'tending to go out every evenin', till the month was up, in a gound zactly like Missus' own (lilock, with seven flounces)—well, jist when I was on the pint o' naming the word, I think'd o' little Ned Pest; and, as I loved the dear little fellow more than a paltry frock, I con'scended to stay!" Here the gardening-groom at the "Snuggery," opposite, grinned and winked horribly, observing something about little Ned's being a "surfeit of finery"—finery that had to be shown and aired,—airing begetting the society of aubun viskers and hofficer X, 50!—officers, making Mr. "Snuggery" chuckle amazingly, and grin more—observing hofficers to be all the "kick" now!—At the same time, jerking his thumb in the direction of the party-wall and the Albert, saying, he knew the Captain,—met *Boultoff* at Bath, where he stayed last season, until the waters were too hot, when he "dried up" (we suppose by drying up, the "Snuggery" meant departed). No one appeared to notice the different name applied to the Captain—or, if they did, said nothing,—except Cook, who observed—her master and the Capting to be as thick as soup!—That she thought the former green and soft, as over-done spinach, for the Capting cut it very fat at master's 'spense;—the guvenor ought to save his bacon afore he be done to rags;—if missus ud come in for all the grizzle, she (cook) said she would not stew and fry herself about it.

"THE HYPOCRIPPLE (YOU DON'T SAY SO!
YES, I PREDICATE HIM TO BE AN HUMBUG?

Poor John, now fully assured of the Captain's intention, is very uncomfortable, indeed; experiencing the combined sensations of goose-skin, fever, pins-and-needles, live-blood, and intoxication—sensations that might have been relieved could they have vanished at the extremities of his hair; but, unfortunately, that would not stand erect, so plastered and powdered had it been since the Captain's arrival. John ruminates upon what has been said, intending to mention the "unmentionables," and break the awful mystery to Mr. Brown, that very night. Now, you must know, Mr. Brown and his friend, the Captain, condescended to grace the juvenile party:—they sat at an occasional table, in the recess, drinking wine, as if for a wager—trying to dispose of all the surplus decanted yesterday; so, you may suppose, when John appeared with a melancholy face, to impart melancholy news, Mr. Brown was too far gone to comprehend it—that night he could not stand, much more understand; though, somehow, under the inspiration of a draught of water and a damp towel, the Diary was made up, as if by instinct:—

"January 5th, *Saturday*.—Christmas is dead!—Expired with the Juvenile party—we have economically disposed of the scraps. 'A Merry Christmas!'—All the *ill luck* came upon Fridays—we can have no more this season—altogether, a jolly Christmas, with a jolly friend, who is to prove himself a *capital* one to-morrow—owes me £350—bill due Monday,—says he will *clear off all by then!* If 'money' is said to be a 'friend,' what must a *friend* with *money* be?—A golden treasure, doubly dear—a companion that can never be a drag, because too well off."

Thus closes the Christmas portion of the Brown Diary:—its author, as customary on Saturday, dyeing his hair, before retiring to rest. But, somehow, that eventful evening, Brown could not repose in peace; he abused his best friends in sleep—dreaming the De Camps capable of decamping, after the bridal breakfast, with the dowry, across the sea—leaving Jemima and Angelina married vestals,—to make more money and fresh conquests in *Virginia* or *Marryland*:—whither old Brown feels bound to follow, in his night shirt, but is incapacitated, being tied to the earth by a pigtail springing from the organs of amativeness, philoprogenitiveness, inhabitiveness, and adhesiveness! So exciting is Brown's dream, that he fancies the De Camps escaping—now, the banging door of the Albert fairly awakening the sleeper; who, on attempting to rise, finds the pillow really a fixture to the back of his head; which he tears away, in a rage, causing all the pleasing sensations that might be experienced on the removal of a tail by the roots. Brown rushes wildly to the window, opening the casement; and, upon looking into the pitch-dark night, he receives a blow from without, that causes him to stagger and reel backwards, falling to the floor, with a noise that makes Mrs. Brown rise in a fright, obtain a light, and severely reprimand her lord as a drunken fool—capable of any wild fancy!

The naked truth stands thus:—Poor Brown has mistaken a bottle of gum for hair-dye, and a closet for the casement—bruising his forehead against the shelf; so, he creeps back to bed—there to lie, moralizing upon cause and effect!—Thinking, how trifling things, in themselves, may lead to disastrous consequences—reflecting upon the rival bottles:—one black—all deceit, the other white and trusty! "Be not precipitate, nor trust to appearances only, lest you be deceived!"—a maxim, Brown fears, he cannot apply to the Captain; for, never did he know less of a man, of whom he ought to have known more.

The 5th of January seemed to Brown as if it would never dawn!—The bump that took away and restored his senses, or, rather, sobered that gentleman, feels like an egg placed in the centre of his forehead—he longs for daylight, to examine it:—daylight, that comes, and reduces the egg to a walnut-shell!—Poor Brown's hat will not go on, for the excrescence, so he cannot go to church. At breakfast he recounts his dream—which is voted fudge by Mamma, stuff by Angelina, and rubbish by Jemima; for they are in no very good humour after the excitement of last week. Little Tom is in bed, having broken his fast upon jalap, administered to counteract the baneful effects of the sweets consumed yesterday— the youth being full as a sack of sand; and, we think, could an anatomist have given a section of the different strata of food that body contained, in the spirit of a geologist, he would have presented a remarkable series of deposits. But, away with scientific speculations, to the Browns, who are at breakfast— a meal that has been intruded upon by John; who has recounted enough of a certain story to put Jemima in hysterics, and Angelina in a fainting fit—bringing down a hurricane of abuse upon him—John, the impertinent menial—John, the venomous viper, that has recoiled upon its benefactor—John, the dark villain, that has plotted with the unworthy man, Spohf, who, of course, out of mere envy, mere spite, mere jealousy, would try to overturn that harmony that is not to be broken so easily—that unity that is not to be severed, no, not for a hundred Spohfs! "Go—go, sir, to your fiddling garret-friend—go and blow his hurdigurdy!—Go, sir!— Tell him the affections of innocent females are not to be played upon like a *base vile*!—Tell him there are ears to pull, horsewhips to be had, ay, and noble gentlemen ever ready to lay on in defence of those scandalously reviled! You may tremble, sir, for menials can be discharged, and have characters to lose! Sir, I give you warning!—Sir, you may go!—Go, sir!"

Now, this is the very thing John much wished to do:—he had been imperceptibly backing, for the last five minutes, towards the door, fearing to turn tail upon the enemy—the choleric Mr. and Mrs.

Brown; who appeared, in their very fierceness, to counteract each other's fire—each pulling the other back, seeming to get more and more ferocious the nearer their victim gained the door,—for, when the baited John reached it, he turned the handle of the lock behind him, still facing his antagonists, intending to escape by a side lurch; but, just at that critical point, there came a knock of great importance at the outer door, as if the chimney were on fire, or a baby half out of window:—the enemy fell back—John opened the door, and, lo!—There discovered an officer of the Police Force, who wanted a word with John Brown!—John, feeling himself the Brown wanted, retreats into the kitchen, where he faints away, in a plate-basket, and stops the Dutch clock.

******

The Police Officer has had his word, or rather, word of words, with Mr. Brown:—news, said to be important, but of the wildest and most improbable character—news, appearing to that gentleman beyond all belief—news, that he will not, can not, put faith in!—Allegations, so preposterous, that they may be disproved in a moment—"Captain de Camp, *alias* Boultoff, &c., &c., and three other persons, names unknown, now incarcerated in Dover Jail, for the robbery of John Brown, of Mizzlington"—a mistake—a foul plot—a base fiction!—At least, so thought the worthy gentleman, who was as ignorant of any wrong done him as the lunatic that resides in the moon. Had the sea-serpent been discovered in the back pond, a gold-mine been found in the dust-bin, or a Sphinx and Centaur been captured in Lincoln's Inn Fields, Mr. Brown could not have been more astounded!—He knows it to be an imputation that can be disproved in a twinkling, if Mr. Police Inspector will just step next door with him; but, alas!—There the fox's tail is left in the trap—the skirt of the very coat, borrowed of Mr. Brown, a fortnight since, hangs in the door,—the very door that slammed, when the affrighted gentleman awoke in a dream, last night.

******

The concluding facts of these eventful sixteen days are simply as follows:—to Mr. Spohf is the issue due—he was bound to spend the sabbath at Canterbury, with the cathedral and organ; upon the journey thither, he happened to recognise some fellow-travellers, better known to him than he was to them. From a slight conversation that transpired, he learned their destination to be Boulogne, or rather, Dover; so he stopped at Ashford, telegraphing their persons to Dover, where, upon arrival, they were provided with lodging free of expense; from that place news was instantly sent to Mizzlington. Little did Mr. Brown think, that morning, as he combed out his matted, gummy, locks, that his friend Captain de Camp had lost *his*, under the cruel shears, in Dover Jail!

******

******

******

Captain de Camp, as you may suppose, after these lucky stars, again entered upon foreign service; being ordered to New South Wales, for fourteen years—he sailed in the same transport with his two sons. Lady Lucretia stayed at home, leading a very retired life—she resided in a vast mansion at the "West-end," a castle at Millbank.

Mr. Spohf, of course, taking advantage of his rival's absence, wins upon Miss Jemima Brown—in the end, marrying her, to live happy ever afterwards?—No, such was not the case! Mr. Spohf espoused Miss Cecilia Lark, who blessed him with a large family and everything else that woman can. Spohf's means have increased, annually, with his family:—all are musical, and the eldest girl is to be an "English Lark," that will surpass the "Swedish Nightingale," or any other foreign bird—the continentalists attribute it to the southern origin of her papa; and, accordingly, claim Cecilia Spohf as their own.

The Misses Brown still remain open to offers, and are reported to be well *worth* having. Mr. John Brown, Junr., is married to Miss Gay; a better *match* there could not be—they both pull one way; but, unfortunately the wrong one—rumour says they are extravagant. Tom is at Westminster School; he has not distinguished himself in any particular study, unless it be boating:—they say he would have won in the last race had he not broken his scull—a mishap that sadly terrified Mrs. Brown; for the note, intimating the catastrophe, said nothing about the *sculls* being more wooden than her son's. Mr. and Mrs. Brown are really very happy!—Victoria and Albert are now united—the party-wall is removed. Mr. B. has retired from business, not even discounting bills:—he does not go to the city now; or at least if he does, it is behind Mr. Strap, who makes an important coachman, having filled out amazingly— may be, thinking, "he who drives fat cattle should himself be fat;" for the bays are too corpulent to kick, and take the journeys at their own pace. John—John Brown, "*private*," now keeps a public house—"the Brown Arms," "the Rampant Locomotive," "Noted Brown Stout House," at the corner of Brown Terrace:—it was a beer-shop when John first took it, but he has since obtained a *licence*, and married Mary, the house-maid.

Mr. Brown is notorious for keeping up the festive Christmas season!—He now makes it a rule to invite only those he loves or respects—not because they are well-to-do in this world, but because he likes or admires them;—seeming fully assured of Time's progress, and that—

CHRISTMAS COMES BUT ONCE A YEAR!

The End